'Chris Goodchild's book  inspiration into the proces: and universal wisdom th of personal trauma and th. functioning autism". His contemplative quest towards becoming at ease with what is, without denying the pain of facing what is in the way of that, is focussed by and within the eternal sky of truth and light. His sixty meditations bring into alignment a cloud of witnesses from many spiritual and philosophical traditions and practices, in true Quaker style, lifting the personal into the universal and honouring the place where words end. There are nine mesmerising illustrations by Julie Lonneman which help to ground the sequence of inner and outer travels and increase the spaciousness of the journey. For me it is a book to read slowly, maybe over a year, honouring the contemplative path and the intense practice in everyday life that leads to "effortless effort", to becoming "unclouded". I will heartily treasure and recommend this luminous book.'

– *Marian Partington, author of* If You Sit Very Still

'With a wisdom honed by transformative pain, Christopher Goodchild invites us to suffuse our lives with a spacious consciousness from which to engage with what is. A moving, beautiful and profoundly truthful book.'

– *Jennifer Kavanagh, author of* The World is Our Cloister *and* A Little Book of Unknowing *of related interest*

Highly Sensitive People in an Insensitive World
How to Create a Happy Life
Ilse Sand
Translated by Elisabeth Svanholmer
ISBN 978 1 78592 066 0
eISBN 978 1 78450 324 6

Re-enchanting the Activist
Spirituality and Social Change
Keith Hebden
ISBN 978 1 78592 041 7
eISBN 978 1 78450 295 9

Spirituality and the Autism Spectrum
Of Falling Sparrows
Abe Isanon
ISBN 978 1 84310 026 3
eISBN 978 0 85700 178 8

Autism and Spirituality
Psyche, Self and Spirit in People on the Autism Spectrum
Olga Bogdashina
ISBN 978 1 84905 285 6
eISBN 978 0 85700 591 5

If You Sit Very Still
Marian Partington
Foreword by Marina Cantacuzino
ISBN 978 1 78592 140 7
eISBN 978 1 78450 407 6

Unclouded *by* Longing

Meditations on Autism and Being Present
in an Overwhelming World

Christopher Goodchild

Foreword by Thomas Moore
With illustrations by Julie Lonneman

Jessica Kingsley *Publishers*
London and Philadelphia

First published in 2017
by Jessica Kingsley Publishers
73 Collier Street
London N1 9BE, UK
and
400 Market Street, Suite 400
Philadelphia, PA 19106, USA

www.jkp.com

Library of Congress Cataloging in Publication Data
A CIP catalog record for this book is available from the Library of Congress

British Library Cataloguing in Publication Data
A CIP catalogue record for this book is available from the British Library

ISBN 978 1 78592 122 3
eISBN 978 1 78450 386 4

Printed and bound in Great Britain

MIX
Paper from responsible sources
FSC
www.fsc.org
FSC® C013604

For Joseph.

There was never a time when you and I did not exist,
...nor will there come a time when we will cease to be.

Bhagavad Gita

Contents

When you make the two one, and when
  you make the inner as the outer
and the outer as the inner...
then you shall enter [the kingdom].

  Gospel of Thomas

Foreword

Christopher Goodchild writes his beautiful book addressing himself as 'you'. I'd like to write some opening words addressing 'you' the reader.

No doubt you've read many books in your lifetime. This one stands out. You'll want to put it on a special shelf that you keep nearby. It is written skilfully and thoughtfully. It has a remarkable feel of originality and speaks to you with a voice that is genuine, not a distant author's tone. The prose is sparkling in its clarity. Christopher's years of reflection have given him a gentle intelligence that he shares in this blend of perennial wisdom and personal insight.

The quotations from the world's spiritual literature are not window dressing. Read them carefully and slowly. Learn from them to study many different classic sources of insight and use them as a daily guide.

Best of all, Christopher's understanding is exceptional. No platitudes or pious restatement of popular 'wisdom'. His insights have been lived and reflected upon and ground to a powder of real profundity. You'll want to read this book, as I have, more than once.

Christopher's memories of growing up with autism will stir your heart and make you wince, but they turn the whole experience inside out, showing the many paradoxes and reversals that are signs of deep understanding. You may feel as I did that Christopher's descriptions of his experiences of living with high-functioning autism sound vaguely familiar. I asked myself more than once, 'Do I have some autistic traits in me?' Is it that, for people outside the

autism spectrum, it is more a seed of character? Could it
be that Christopher's autism was his gift, allowing him
to write such a penetrating and true book? (What I mean
here is what a carpenter might mean by a true angle –
sharp, exact, skilfully done.)

In his book Christopher dialogues with sages of the
past and appreciates their improbable and contrary ways
of seeing and wording things. Do you realise that you live
in an odd world, where most people seem to live on the
surface, believing in the common logic and values that
surround them, whilst the great teachers are always seeing
a mirror land of opposite, more transcendent values?
That's why I place Lewis Carroll and Alice's adventures
among the basic spiritual texts, and why I felt thrilled
to find a beautiful translation of Rilke in Christopher's
book, a poet who encourages you to listen to the Orphic
song that comes from underground and that offers you an
alternative reality.

The book you are reading is a spiritual book in the best
meaning of the word 'spiritual'. Here's how Christopher
defines it, addressing himself: 'Spirituality for you has
little to do with beliefs, but in living faithfully within the
mystery of what it means to be most human.' This is a
good start to a definition, and the book as a whole shows
how to be spiritual in a real way. I am happy to say that
there is no sentimentality in this book that could contain a
ton of it. It presents the spiritual as real, not wistful or rosy.

I see the spiritual as the edge of your experience, where
you sense the mysterious and all that lies beyond your
limited understanding. It opens a gate in your materialism
and subjectivity, allowing a taste of the vast unseen and
the timeless. It extends your knowing so that you can deal
intelligently with grief and hopelessness. These appear as

enemies and immovable obstacles when you fence yourself within the superficial thoughts of a materialistic society.

This book will help you take on life as it presents itself without surrendering to depression. You may already have put up with people who criticise you and abuse you. Christopher shows you how to shift to a position where you don't accept that abuse and don't set yourself up for more of it. He talks about the soul, one of my favourite words, and shows you how to care for yourself at such a deep and radical level that you become immune to the ignorant taunts of the world. You live your own life and enjoy transcendent standards.

Don't read this book at a distance. Take it home, deep into your heart. Be radicalised by it for your soul. Be fully in your world, but follow the laws of a much vaster world, one that can be known and cherished only mysteriously. That is the meaning of religion, though that word has been reduced to organisations and creeds. You live in the world but always keep your eyes on a higher level. The tragedies of life succumb to healing only when an alternative, more transcendent and sublime point of view plays a serious part in your understanding.

You may carry emotional injuries from a harsh parent or an unenlightened teacher. Or, like Christopher, you may have congenital problems. These wounds can be painful and can interrupt the peace of your life and inhibit your hopes. But they can also be the crack in your cosmos that allows life to pour in.

This extraordinary book gives you trustworthy and comprehensive guidelines. Read it slowly, again and again, making it your own. Let it inspire your own way and your own principles. Be encouraged to make your life matter in spite of all obstacles.

Thomas Moore

Author of Care of the Soul

Acknowledgements

I would like to thank the following people, whose valuable contributions to this book are warmly and gratefully acknowledged:

Katherine, who has accompanied me during the whole process of writing this book and editing it with me

Brian, for all his indispensable technical assistance throughout, and in preparing the manuscript

Sylvaine, for her meticulous help with sourcing and listing the quotations for the reference section, together with the wonderful support she has shown me

Julie, for her beautiful illustrations, particularly as this is the second time she has agreed to work with me in illustrating my books

Friends' House, Euston Road, for offering a sanctuary of calm and shelter in which to reflect and work on the book

Thomas Moore, for his generous praise in his very perceptive foreword, and Jennifer Kavanagh and Marian Partington, for their complimentary and thoughtful endorsements

The authors who have kindly given me permission to use quotations from their work – Rex Ambler, Danna Faulds, Dorothy Hunt, Danelle LaFlower, Thomas Moore and Rashani Réa

All the teachers and authors who have inspired me in the writing of this book, such as Ramana Maharshi, Jesus, Ram Dass, Henri Nouwen, Tara Brach and Thich Nhat Hanh, to name but a few

All the friends who have accompanied me throughout this time of writing

And finally, Natalie, at Jessica Kingsley Publishers, for inviting me to write this book in the first place.

As Ram Dass said, 'we're all just walking each other home.' How true! And how we do so in the most unexpected ways.

Introduction

The fifth-century poet and philosopher Lao Tzu is often quoted as saying, 'Truth waits for eyes unclouded by longing', the inspiration behind the title of this book.

Over the years, I have come to interpret this statement not as a denial of longing, for it is longing that makes us most human. Instead, I have come to see that by not allowing overwhelming desires or circumstances to obscure our true nature, we are able to affirm our deepest humanity, the spark of eternity within us all.

I see the spiritual journey as a continuous unfolding into the truth of who we really are. Being most human, which invariably means being most vulnerable, then becomes a script for the awakening of a deeper and more authentic spirituality. My own spiritual quest has led me to the sages, poets and mystics of many paths, both East and West. In turn, this led me to adopt contemplative practice, the natural language of which is silence, as the means of creating distance and finding perspective within the multitude of sensory and psychological dramas I have experienced, and continue to work through, in my life.

My intense longing to share silence with others was to eventually lead me to the Quakers, and their values of peace, equality, truth and simplicity. It is here in recent years that I have found a true home, where I can move freely, beyond words, ritual and creedal definition, and into the formless direct experience of the divine. In the Quaker meeting for worship I am often reminded of Krishnamurti's statement about truth: 'Truth is a pathless land... Truth, being limitless, unconditioned, unapproachable by any path whatsoever, cannot be organized...' My own experience has taught me too that, however compelling theology and religious practice may be, these things can never lead me to truth. There is something about the quality of the gathered silence in a Quaker meeting for worship that moves me to a deeper dimension – the heart.

In 2007, I was diagnosed with high-functioning autism. Like many on the autism spectrum, I lived much of my life being socially marginalised and feeling quite at home on the fringes of society. However, I no longer feel an outsider. In fact, in many ways I feel an insider, for life's events alongside having autism have played their part in taking me deeper, beyond the surface and superficialities of life. Although much of my life has not been easy, I can now say that my insights have led me beyond 'inside' or 'outside', beyond 'self' and 'other', beyond brokenness.

In the same way in which the French philosopher and mystic, Pierre Teilhard de Chardin, once said, 'We are not human beings having a spiritual experience, but spiritual beings having a human experience,' I could equally say that I am a spiritual being having a human experience of which autism is an integral part. For whilst autism is a part of the way I am, it is not who 'I am'. Who 'I am' is way beyond the remit of neurology, psychology and the constraints and limitations of mainstream religion. When seen through spiritual eyes there is no separation whatsoever between psychology, philosophy, neurology, spirituality – all are interconnected and can never be separated from the spiritual journey. Everything is as one. It is from this perspective that I document my reflections in this book.

Nearly a decade ago I wrote a book about my experiences called *A Painful Gift: The Journey of a Soul with Autism*, which concluded with me pondering on such questions as, 'How much have I loved?' and, 'How much have I forgiven?' Today, almost ten years since I wrote those words, I would add, 'How much have I been present, both within myself and with those I love?' For if I have not been present, who is there that is really loving, and who is there that is really forgiving? It is out of this questioning that the reflections in this book, *Unclouded by Longing*, were born, as I attempted to convey my desire to be more present and affirm my true nature in a wide variety of situations in my everyday life.

This book takes the form of a collection of 60 meditations that, with the exception of the last one, are written in the second person, in the form of an inner dialogue or tête-à-tête with myself. Writing in the 'you' is not only powerful but also helpful, as it creates a direct and objective approach that avoids getting wrapped up in the details and missing the bigger picture. The themes I have covered are universally applicable and will be of interest to anyone who is drawn to contemplative spirituality. Themes such as love and loss, doubt and faith, as well as psychological trauma, alienation, prayer, depression and anxiety are all thoroughly explored. There is also a more light-hearted side to some of the narratives that reflects my love of humour, playfulness and idiosyncratic ways. Laughter simply creates a space for grace.

It is my hope that these writings, together with the beautiful and inspirational illustrations by Julie Lonneman that enhance the book, may inspire you to draw deeply from the well of wisdom that resides within you.

An invisible and subtle essence is the
spirit of the whole universe.
That is reality. That is truth. Thou Art That.

Chandogya Upanishad

1

Unclouded by Longing

Truth waits for eyes unclouded by longing.

Lao Tzu

'With original fear comes original desire,' says the Vietnamese Zen master Thich Nhat Hanh. If this is true, and you have no reason to doubt his wisdom, then your earliest experiences of emotional neglect and deprivation set you up for abundant suffering and longing, over and above the fear every human being experiences at the time of their birth.

However, you see your life like a continuously flowing river that has carried you from denial of suffering, to attachment to suffering, and then into the awareness of witnessing the entire drama of your life, in order to see it simply as a script for your awakening.

This has not been an easy journey, and it has rarely been as straightforward as it sounds. However, you have been fortunate to have had, and continue to have, many wise guides who have directed you along the way. Each loving guide has assisted you in seeing that suffering can not only break you down, it can also break you open, revealing to you the deepest part of your humanity – your soul.

Time and time again, and in so many ways, intense suffering has proven to be the necessary prerequisite for the next degree of consciousness to come through. The wise Sufi saying, 'As the heart grieves for what it has lost, the spirit laughs for what it has found,' resonates deeply within you.

In the same way that you can use your mind to overcome your mind, you can equally use longing to overcome longing, that is if you ask, with an open heart, what it is that you truly long for. Your answer to that potent question is always the same – you are already what you long for.

When you understand it, when you really understand it, not just in your intellect, but in the bones of your being, that there is no separation between you and absolutely everything, which includes the divine, then the game changes. No longer are you swimming like a fish in the ocean of existence, going round and round in circles saying, 'Where, O where is the ocean?' For now, you can see, and with ever greater clarity, that you and the ocean are one. There are clouds, for you are human, but the clouds no longer obscure the deeper reality of your true, timeless and unchanging nature.

2

What Is It You Truly Long for?

Thou hast made us for thyself, O Lord, and our heart is restless until it finds its rest in thee.

St Augustine of Hippo

Some years ago now, you met a Benedictine monk who had left the monastery in order to live the life of an anchorite in the city of Norwich. Following in the footsteps of the 14th-century mystic, Julian of Norwich, this quiet unassuming man drew you deeper into the contemplative life in a way that you could never have foreseen.

Each day he would sit all alone in the small cell attached to the very same church Julian would have sat in over 600 years before. Like Julian he would offer counsel to anyone who sought him out, be they pilgrim, tourist or anybody in need.

There was something about this man's presence that instantly attracted you, and after a brief conversation between you both, you were left with little doubt that he would be your teacher. Twice a week you would visit him, sitting in complete silence together, until you felt called to share with him what was in your heart. Never before had you felt listened to with such love. Here the sublime words of the American Quaker, Douglas Steer, come immediately to mind. 'To "listen" another's soul into a condition of disclosure and discovery may be almost the greatest service that any human being ever performs for another.' To be seen at such depth was life-changing.

One day, out of the silence, you said, 'I have always felt this insatiable sense of longing, so vast, so powerful, that at times it feels that I will be totally overcome.' His response was quite spontaneous, 'What is it you truly long for?' Never before had a question aroused such intense curiosity and affected you so deeply.

This simple question stayed with you. Asking, 'What is it you truly long for?', spontaneously and with an open heart, has become a powerful way of using your mind to move beyond your mind and into the deeper Self that the question would indirectly instruct. It would in time play its part in moving you beyond the concept of who you imagined yourself to be, and into the deeper reality of who you really are.

A year or so after your first encounter with the monk he fell seriously ill, and was no longer able to accompany you in the capacity in which you had become accustomed. However, his presence never left you, for he is always in your heart. As is the question he posed all those years ago, 'What is it you truly long for?'

3

The Light behind the Watcher

Be still and cool in thy own mind and spirit from thy own thoughts...

George Fox

You have autism – but it is not who you are. Who you are is way beyond neurology, psychology and genetics. Who you are is beyond who you think or believe yourself to be.

You see yourself as a spiritual being having a human experience of which autism is an integral part. All of these factors contribute to you feeling as though you are living in between two very contrasting worlds, the autistic world and the neurologically 'typical' world. This 'in-between' space, this being in the world but not quite at home within it, can often feel excruciatingly lonely, exhausting and uncomfortable. However, it can also be a place of enormous creativity and insight. Often you feel as though you are living on the threshold of something vital and new, experiencing your human journey with such vibrant and enthusiastic curiosity, where each day can feel like a rite of passage in itself.

You have found a very special home in the Quakers (the Religious Society of Friends), whose natural home is silence and the Light that is found within. In a Quaker meeting for worship you step off the stage and drama of life and enter into a very different dimension. Here silence becomes like a screen upon which the movies of your life are played out. Your thoughts, feelings and memories become like images on a movie reel that are being projected by the light of awareness. Your challenge is to affirm with deep loving-kindness the humanness inherent within the drama, whilst at the same time shifting your awareness to your identification with the Light itself.

'As you watch your mind,' said Nisargadatta, 'you discover your self as the watcher. When you stand motionless, only watching, you discover your self as the light behind the watcher.'

4

The Quaker Way

Take heed, dear Friends, to the promptings of love and truth in your hearts.

Quaker Faith and Practice

In so many ways you have always been a natural Quaker, and amongst 'Friends' you have found a very natural home.

Whilst you have the utmost respect for other paths, whose creeds, prayer forms and rituals have held you firmly in the past, you have in later life needed a little more space to move and breathe in every area of your life, in particular in the areas of belief and corporate worship.

Looking back now you can see that the creeds and practices you followed were like oars of a boat that helped you cross this ocean of existence. Although they served you well, and for this you will always be grateful, what serves you better now is the silence.

As a young man, these opening lines from Rimbaud's poem, 'The Drunken Boat', captured your imagination: 'I drifted on a river I could not control, no longer guided by the bargemen's ropes.' For you today, they capture perfectly your freedom to be guided simply by your conscience and experience alone. This, allied with God's grace, is the Quaker way. This has become your way. It is here, in this Quaker space, you dwell among fellow travellers.

The Quaker way holds naturally both the contemplative and the activist. Often it seems to you that spirituality can so easily become concerned with one of two alternatives, to the exclusion of the other – either engaging with the drama of the world at the expense of the Self, or engaging with the Self at the expense of the world. In contrast, the Quaker way, inspired by Jesus, is to hold in balance both the 'being' and the 'doing'.

Refining this dance of being and doing is for you of great importance. However, this is not an easy path, as there will be times when you will need to receive more, and times when you will be called to give more. The silence of a Quaker meeting for worship is often a perfect space to make a discernment on such issues.

Community can be problematic for you, as you get easily overwhelmed by social interaction. However, whenever you step into meeting for worship, you feel as though you have come in from the cold. This is not just because there is a political, intellectual and spiritual affinity, but because there is an integrated way of being that is often palpable within Quakers and the Quaker way itself. This naturally draws you deeper into the Quaker way of life and the Quaker values of Peace, Equality, Truth and Simplicity. These values resonate with you deeply.

This is a way of life. This has now become *your* life.

5

The Sorrowful Price of Freedom

I saw also that there was an ocean of darkness and death,
but an infinite ocean of light and love, which flowed over the
ocean of darkness...

George Fox

Much of your early life was deeply traumatic. Having a strongly creative side to your nature, as well as having high-functioning autism, enabled you to adapt so skilfully to the world, whilst at the same time feeling almost completely alienated from it. The extent to which you were daily humiliated and abused for your unusual ways and practices became the extent to which you were to conceal your pain and your natural way of relating to yourself and others. Too powerless to fight and too young to take flight, you simply froze, and a steel-like armour formed around your heart.

This protective armouring became like a seamless garment you wore, until the gift of desperation had you falling apart. Then grief, like an all-consuming river, pulled you deeper and deeper into its powerful undercurrents. Here you learned what powerlessness really meant. You lost the person you thought you were, whilst being swept into an ocean of overwhelming sadness. Grief was to become the means of purification, cleansing you from the inside out, taking you out of your mind and into your heart. 'There is nothing so whole as a broken heart,' goes the old Hebrew saying.

How strange it is that we humans rail against the very things that can set us free...such as grief. Your grief was so deep that it remained hidden away beneath the surface, until the conditions were right for it to be expressed. The residue of past hurts is often evoked through life's events. However, today you are able to put spacious awareness around the grief of your past, in order for it to intrude less into the present.

The important role played by grief was highlighted by Henri Nouwen, who said, 'Grief is the discipline of the heart...and knows itself to be the sorrowful price of freedom without which love cannot bloom.'

The ocean of darkness is overcome by the light and love within you – that is if you have faith to allow it to be so. Grief has given you eyes to see and the freedom to be who you really are.

6

Befriending Your 'Black Dog'

Art thou in Darkness?
Mind it not, for if thou dost it will fill thee more,
but stand still and act not, and wait in patience
till Light arise from Darkness to lead thee.

James Nayler

Your thoughts can often feel as though they conspire against you without your awareness, let alone your consent. It is as though depression has its own key and it lets itself in through the back door, taking up residence within your very soul.

However, your thoughts are like seeds, wholesome and unwholesome, within the interior garden of your mind. Your job is to discern what seeds you wish to grow through the watering can of attention. For you have taken it upon yourself to become an interior gardener. Here you have a choice as to whether you grow seeds that will produce beautiful flowers, or weeds that will strangle the life out of you.

This watchfulness over your thoughts is so important in overcoming the 'Black Dog' of depression, for to be negligent in this respect can have serious consequences. On the surface, it seems that your Black Dog is a hungry sabre-toothed monster that seeks to devour you and tear you apart. However, the reality could not be further from the truth, for this Black Dog is that part of you which you unconsciously pushed away into the shadowlands of your being a long, long time ago – your inner child. The extent to which you can hold tenderly your Black Dog will become the extent to which its true face can be revealed.

Often it feels as though your inner child has taken up residence within the small, tight and contracted space within and around the labyrinth of your heart. Over many years, you have felt your inner child's coldness, agitation, rage, despair and utter powerlessness. What remains is an ocean of sadness and grief, which is often evoked through the passing of the seasons and through the events that continue to unfold in your life.

With your hand on your heart, you breathe into the tight and contracted area around your chest and whisper, 'I can see you. You are safe. We are no longer separate. We breathe as one, and I love you.'

7

Allowing Your Body
to Speak Its Mind

Be strong then, and enter into your own body...

Kabir

As well as being on the autism spectrum you also have deep psychological scars, but whilst trauma remains a fact of life for you, it does not have to be a life sentence.

Often it is difficult for you to differentiate between what is a traumatic response and what is an autistic reaction to simply being overwhelmed. However, when you are able to slow down and witness your fleeting thoughts, as opposed to being swept up in them, you are able to see a clearer picture. In such spacious awareness you can see that your thoughts and patterns of reactivity associated with your autism often have a lesser charge to them, compared with thoughts that are attached to trauma. Thoughts commonly associated with sensory overload include 'This is so overwhelming, I feel as though I'm going to die,' whereas those thoughts associated with a traumatic reaction would be 'This is so overwhelming I believe I am dying.'

Much of your adult life has been spent acquiring the skills of challenging unhelpful beliefs and lovingly re-parenting yourself. Since your body remembers what your mind has had to forget, much of this loving re-parenting involves listening to your body and holding tenderly the distress that your body is communicating, and then releasing into the experience it embodies. In listening deeply to your body, you are learning to transform patterns of traumatic reactivity. This takes enormous skill, as does the tender holding of that part of you that suffered in the past. All this enables the movement from compassionately holding into compassionately witnessing, both of which run concurrently.

Your body is the wisest of teachers. Allow your body to speak its mind and listen deeply to what it has to say.

8

Giving In but Not Giving Up

Whether 'tis nobler in the mind to suffer
The slings and arrows of outrageous fortune,
Or to take arms against a sea of troubles...

William Shakespeare

You have never wanted to end your life, though there have been times when you wanted so desperately to kill the pain within you.

Just before your diagnosis with high-functioning autism, you were suffering from severe depression. A lifetime of unrelentingly swimming against the tide left you exhausted, alienated and existentially questioning the value of surviving any longer in a world that was forever beyond your grasp.

A part of you was horrified that you could even contemplate taking your life, because of how much suffering this would cause your son as well as others who love you. Yet your suffering became so intense you were fast becoming insulated from the pain you would cause others. You had philosophically worked out how everyone would be better off without you. You simply felt that suicide was the kindest thing you could do – you saw it as an act of compassion. You gave yourself a week to get your act together and set the date for a week's time when you would make your quiet and dignified exit.

However, before this could happen, you stumbled onto something you had not planned. Part of getting your 'act' together turned out to be giving up your 'act' completely, in fact, giving up being the actor altogether. For the first time in your life you gave yourself permission to stop fighting and just let go. The effect this had on you was quite extraordinary. Tension just fell from your body, as did this chronic sense of feeling alienated and separate from the world. Everything became illuminated in this your 'last week'. People, places, things – all had a charge and energy that pulsated through your veins. You just let go.

During this time you started writing a journal. At first you had thought this would be a long suicide note, offering some kind of detailed explanation as to why life was so unendurable. However, a new thought now plagued you that perhaps life might be just bearable if somehow you could continue to experience even a mere fraction of this release and 'letting go' into life that you were now experiencing. But how?

It felt as though you had been given a stay of execution, and into this very new space a seed of light was found within you. You called this seed by many names – consciousness, awareness, the Light, even God. But what really mattered wasn't what you called it, but the faithfulness with which you called upon it.

What followed was that you opened yourself to the process of psychological and spiritual guidance, and slowly you developed a new perception of the interior landscape within you. You saw how this inner landscape was overgrown with weeds of despair and fear. These unwholesome seeds had grown strong through your inability to see how you were unconsciously nurturing them by giving them undue attention.

As never before, you came to see that the 'battleground' was within. To win this battle was not so much about surviving the experience, but entering into it in a way that would leave you transformed. Slowly you were able to recognise that there was no battle to be fought at all. For it was all about surrendering, surrendering into life. A giving in without a giving up.

9

The World as a Stage

All the world's a stage,
and all the men and women merely players;
They have their exits and their entrances,
and one man in his time plays many parts.

William Shakespeare

You are not a writer or teacher, you are a being, *being* a writer and a teacher. Whenever you identify with the roles you play out in life, you fall prey to a case of mistaken identity.

However, all attempts to abandon being human in pursuit of being spiritual will equally be flawed, for this will only leave a ghostly shadow that will merely create a persona of being spiritual at the cost of authentic transcendence. Spirituality is not about stepping off the stage, completely abandoning your roles and identity. It is about using the stage of life in order to wake up. This is what you understand by Jesus's reference to being in the world but not of the world.

You are a soul passing through a life in which the entire drama is a script for your awakening, or as the philosopher and mystic Pierre Teilhard de Chardin once said, 'We are not human beings having a spiritual experience. We are spiritual beings having a human experience.'

The cinema and movie screen are wonderfully rich metaphors in conveying the interior life. You are in essence the light, and not the interplay of light and shadow that form the images projected upon the screen. As George Fox said, 'The Light is that by which ye come to see,' and the screen within is simply consciousness expanding into awareness itself – God.

Creating a spacious awareness around all the dramas you face in life is quite a challenge, especially when the going gets tough. It is for this reason that you take regular time out each day for meditation and contemplation, even when it is the last thing you want to do.

When the curtain eventually falls on your life, it is highly likely that all your beliefs will fall away from you, like beautifully coloured autumn leaves in the cool autumnal breeze. What remains would be that part of you that is timeless, unchanging and eternal, which is beyond the concept of who you think you are.

Autism and Spirituality

I am a spiritual being on a human journey into which autism is inseparably woven.

Christopher Goodchild

Spirituality for you has little to do with beliefs, but in living faithfully within the mystery of what it means to be most human.

You have little desire for the beliefs in which God, or ultimate reality, is 'wrapped up'. What you truly ache for is what you already are, though you cannot yet fully see this truth. This is because you have more work to do in loosening your attachment to the play of duality that separates you from God, so compelling your roles as father, son, teacher, writer, or even a person on the autism spectrum.

Deep down you know that your true identity is a soul dressed up within these very roles. Here the image of Lazarus comes to mind, for like him, you, too, are being called out of death into life – out of the darkness of ignorance and into the light of awareness. The more you are being drawn out into the light, the more your roles that you wear like tightly wrapped bandages unravel and loosen.

Like many on the autism spectrum, you can be absolutely resolute and relentless when you set your mind to achieving things. Such drivenness and dogged persistence, combined with your ability to hyper-focus, can be a great asset in life. However, whilst you can be driven by obsession and attain your goals in the world, the spiritual life is a completely different game. In the world the emphasis is on how much you can accumulate, whereas in the spiritual life it is about how much you can let go of. Drivenness can only take you so far up the mountain.

This represents an enormous challenge for you, for how can you tell the difference between obsessionality which is so natural for you and many others on the autism spectrum, and the unforced discipline of letting go into the one-pointedness of mind referred to in the Hindu and Buddhist traditions. It is in overcoming this challenge that your vocational calling to the Alexander Technique pays dividends. Through this you have come to understand that whilst obsessionality has a clinging and contracted quality, like a tightly clenched fist, contemplative practice is, by its very nature, soft, expansive and all-embracing, like a releasing and opening hand. The same principle applies with respect to your carefully structured routines, for whilst they can hold and contain you, if taken to the extreme, they can become vice-like and leave no aperture for the light to enter.

The extent to which you can hold tenderly your autism together with all your life's experiences is the extent to which you can move beyond seeing them as an identity and into your deeper nature as a spiritual being.

11

To Love What *Is*

In this choiceless
never-ending
flow
of life,
there is an infinite array
of choices.
One alone
brings happiness –
to love
what is.

Dorothy Hunt

What is, *is*, whether you like it or not. However, how do you wake up to what *is*, when your whole being is in a state of resistance or denial?

Whether you are running away from a painful experience, or simply holding on to an image of yourself that has passed its sell-by date, those wise words from Carl Gustav Jung, 'What you resist persists,' ring out like a Muslim call to prayer. 'Letting be' the thoughts, feelings and memories that move within you is no easy task, but as you become more willing to be present with 'what is', a different quality of attention will emerge.

You set your intention to surrender your life completely to God, and often it seems as though you fail, as worries and the urge to over-plan and control your life take over. However, when you are able to see this whole illusion of control in play, you start waking up to a deeper reality, the reality that you are not the person you believe yourself to be. *You* are not the doer.

In surrendering your life in this way, however imperfectly this is done, a whole new way of perceiving slowly unfolds within you. You feel more alive from the inside out, until the line dividing inside and out simply fades away, enriching not only your physical body, but your soul as well. On one level, the relative dimension, you can see that there is choice and free will, whilst on another level, the ultimate dimension, you can see that there is really no such thing as freedom of choice, and that having control is a complete illusion.

How you hold this duality will greatly influence how far you can find true and lasting peace and simply be with what *is*.

12

Life as a Painful Gift

The cure for pain is in the pain.

Rumi

Since your autobiography *A Painful Gift* was published some years ago, life's events would frequently reopen various painful chapters of the book within you. In many ways, the whole process created something akin to a nervous system, a web of connectivity, whereby you were able to feel feelings that you had previously only been able to grasp intellectually.

Perhaps it is true to say that you have experienced two kinds of suffering; the first resulted in running away from your pain, the second from embracing your pain. The first suffering imprisoned you, whilst the second laid the conditions to set you free. The extent to which you can hold your suffering without undue attachment to it becomes the extent to which you can move beyond the pain and the identification of being its victim. However, this is a lifelong process and you have already travelled some way along this path of healing.

Embracing your suffering has expanded your heart, and in so doing given you eyes to see the suffering of humanity with love and compassion. This work is soul work, and you have been greatly fortunate to have had many wise guides to assist you along this healing journey. Pain becomes gift whenever you are able to use it as an agent to move beyond your small self and into a deeper sense of who you really are.

Helen Keller, the deaf and blind author, understood this well when she wrote, 'I believe that God is in me as the sun is in the colour and fragrance of a flower – the Light in my darkness, the voice in my silence.'

Transforming pain into gift is a process, and contemplative practice is the path that you have whole-heartedly embraced in order to undertake this work. As Zen master Thich Nhat Hanh says, 'Suffering is the kind of mud that we must be able to use in order to grow the flower of understanding and love.' Your life is spent rolling up your sleeves and tending lovingly to this interior garden within, transforming your suffering into a garden of tranquillity.

You have come to see that your life has been all about holding opposites, only to then wake up and see these very opposites as simply different expressions of the oneness that permeates everything.

This is the 'painful gift' that is your life.

13

Autism as a Flower

There are many flowers within the interior garden of my being, and few are as fragrant or as colourful as those of autism.

Christopher Goodchild

To the world in general, autism remains a mystery to be fixed and pitied. To you, autism is a way of being and seeing reality in a very intense and colourful way.

Much of your early life was spent studying the human condition, as opposed to allowing yourself to *be* human. You lived within a 'cloud of unknowing' that you were on the autism spectrum, and as a result you were unconsciously over-adapting to a world that was forever beyond your reach. Your human existence and quality of life were severely compromised by the physical and emotional exhaustion of constantly over-compensating for something you could never give a name to.

You were conditioned to feel ashamed of your routines, idiosyncratic ways, tics, sensory issues and complex ways of processing information. As a result, you pushed into the shadowlands of your being the beautiful flower of autism. Here you remained hidden behind a mask of appearing 'normal', until the mask had served its purpose, and simply fell from your face with the unfrozen tears that had created the mask in the first place.

Diagnosis is such a clinical word to describe a moment in which your humanity is so deeply affirmed, understood and valued. Receiving an official diagnosis of high-functioning autism was not so much like being given a medical label; it was for you a moment of enlightenment.

The process of healing and integration was not easy. It was a complex task affirming what you had been conditioned to believe until then was unacceptable. There was also enormous grief for all those years of being so lost, alone and in the dark.

To see your story as a tragedy, or as one of mere survival, is to completely miss the point. When you can affirm the human drama of it all, yet identify not with the main character but with the soul within the main character, a deeper reality emerges. It is here that no tear or cry of anguish goes unheard. Everything, absolutely everything, is as it should be for your awakening to the divine presence within. For *you* are not living your life; you are being lived *through*.

Today you tend to the flower of autism in your interior garden with love. You celebrate, rather than hide away in shame, your idiosyncratic ways and behaviours, and whilst there are many different kinds of wild and colourful flowers here, few have not been touched by the fragrance of autism.

14

Quaker Meeting for Worship

...the end of words is to bring us to the knowledge of things beyond which words can utter.

Isaac Penington

Quaker meeting for worship offers you a space where you are truly accepted, whilst at the same time being lovingly held in an oasis of calm.

In a world where you often feel buffeted around in an overwhelming sensory ocean of noise, unsettling imagery and stimulation, both externally and internally, the silence of a Quaker meeting for worship is a true refuge. However, there is a deeper meaning to this silence than just a refuge from the world, as it offers you a portal or doorway into another dimension. Here, in the silence, you experience a profound sense of oneness within yourself and with others. It is as though you step off the stage and drama of life, and into a very different dimension altogether.

This temporary stepping off the stage of the world and into the cool stillness of meeting for worship has a timeless quality all of its own. For it is here that you put aside your identity as a father, teacher, writer or person on the autism spectrum, and simply drift without the 'oars' of methods or creeds upon an ocean that carries you to the divine within.

Your experience of community and social groups in the past has been painful, and you have often felt awkward and at times distressed just trying to stay afloat whilst processing copious amounts of information. This always made you feel like an outsider. However, in the silence of a Quaker meeting for worship, you move from being an outsider to being an insider, whereby you are able to experience a sense of equanimity within yourself as well as equality with those around you. There is no more fitting way to convey this experience than through those exquisite words quoted above, from the 17th-century Quaker, Isaac Penington:

> The end of words is to bring us to the knowledge of things beyond which words can utter.

15

The Heart as a Lonely Hunter

The little space within the heart is as great as the vast universe.
The heavens and the earth are there, and the sun and the moon
and the stars...

Chandogya Upanishad

You have lived much of your life on the margins of society, and it is from these very margins that universal truths have been placed upon your heart. The painful gift of being broken so many times has simply enabled these gifts to drop into your heart and colour your whole being.

However, for much of your life you have fought to stay alive and simply remain sane in a world that has exposed you to so much cruelty and humiliation. These experiences were traumatic, harrowing and disturbing, and often left you overwhelmed with such deep sadness.

The extent to which you were deprived of love became the extent to which you would ache for it. In so many ways your experiences teach you that whilst desire is what makes you most human, attachment to desire points you to where your real work remains. It is here that you draw deep inspiration from the great Indian sage Ramana Maharshi when he is quoted as saying, 'There is no happiness in the thing [we desire]. What happens is that your desires were molesting you, it was troubling you, agitating your mind. When you get the thing [you want], the agitation stops, and it is the relief from the agitation that you are interpreting as the joy you are receiving.'

Now you are able to create the conditions whereby you can listen deeply to the traumatised child within you. So much so, that today you can lovingly hold the wounds of your past with greater compassion. This in turn enables you to see things more as they are, and not so much as they appear to be.

Changing the very limited and finite way through which you see your life ultimately will mean challenging belief systems. This work on yourself will, sooner or later, come at a cost, the cost being the death of the person you believed yourself to be. So, whilst you remain clinging to the image you still have of yourself, you merely create distance from your true identity. As the Prophet Muhammad said, 'Each person is only a mask, which the soul puts on for a season. It is worn for the proper time, and then is cast off.'

A useful question to ask yourself is, 'What exactly are you lonely for?' or, 'What is it that your heart really wants?' When you are able to be with such questions in the silence of your heart itself, you are then able to see with eyes unclouded by longing. For your heart is no longer hunting, for seeker and sought are found, not wanting, but as one.

16

What Desire Are You Using to Give Up Desire?

In order to be All, do not desire to be anything.
In order to know All, do not desire to know anything.
In order to find the joy of All, do not desire to enjoy anything.

St John of the Cross

It hardly needs to be said that, without desire, none of us would be here, and you, the reader, would not be reading this now. Desire in itself is just part of what makes you human. However, when you become attached to desire, you enter into a very different game altogether.

As a child, you had great longing to feel safe and to be loved, but these basic human needs were never adequately met. This paved the way for conflict, since you were forever recreating through relationships the early drama of your past, in order to re-enter it in the hope of trying to meet those needs and find healing.

The many ways and means that you attempted, in order to extricate yourself from your attached desires, addictions and unhealthy relationships, proved counter-productive. You simply did not have the level of awareness to trace your longing to its source and ask yourself deeply and with an open heart, 'What desire are you using to give up desire?' or, 'What does this wanting part of you really want?' The answer to these questions takes you deeper, beyond the trying to fix, and into simply being with what is unfolding within you. It is impossible for you to push away an attachment, because that is an attachment too. Attachments simply fall away when the conditions are right. This is beautifully brought home by the well-loved spiritual guide, Ram Dass, when he said, 'You're finished with your desires at the rate you finish your desires. You can't rip the skin off the snake. The snake must moult its skin. That's the rate it happens.'

Contemplative practice for you facilitates the shedding of such a skin, a letting go of the person you believe yourself to be, and the chattering thoughts associated with it. To simply be with everything that passes through your awareness. This is no easy undertaking, for in the same way that the snake undergoes great discomfort, you, too, will have to face the residue of overwhelming fear lurking in your mind. The American novelist Anne Lamott famously said, 'My mind is like a bad neighborhood, I try not to go there alone...' and you understand where she is coming from.

In the silence of a Quaker meeting for worship you find the conditions to shed your 'skin', loosening your attachment to your thinking mind, enabling you to draw from this well of being in your everyday life. In so doing you create more of a spacious awareness around the drama of desire, enabling you to move beyond the drama and into the essence of who you truly are. As Krishna says in the *Bhagavad Gita*, 'If we desire anything for its finite pleasure we shall miss its infinite joy.'

17

The Light Dressed Up
as 'Self' and 'Other'

Thou art imperishable.
Thou art changeless reality.
Thou art the source of life.

Chandogya Upanishad

You have come to see that we are all the Light dressed up as self and other. The one playing the game of being the many.

Waking up to who you really are is a process. It is only when you can liberate yourself from your mind and drop into your heart that you can begin to see that there really is actually no separate self or person there to be awakened in the first place. The more your heart expands, the more you see the play of life like a jigsaw puzzle, in which each piece represents a different aspect of your human journey.

Paradoxically, as the near-completed picture of your human story emerges, a deeper reality is revealed. No longer being preoccupied with trying to figure it all out and hold it all together, you simply let go into the bigger picture from which your story hangs – an all-embracing panoramic view of life in all its entirety – timeless, unchanging and eternal. However, in order to authentically make this movement from your small contracted sense of self and into who you really are, you will need to lovingly hold the entire drama of your human story. This is a work in progress. This is your script for awakening.

Your perception of how you saw yourself was shattered soon after your diagnosis with high-functioning autism. Along with this was a dramatic relinquishing of all your beliefs that had held together your concept of who you believed yourself to be up to that point. It took a little time to integrate this understanding, for it to drop into your being. When it did, and this was no easy process, you simply saw a deeper reality. As the astronomer Arthur Eddington once said, 'Something unknown is doing we don't know what.'

This cosmic dance of being the Light dressed up and disguised as self and other is compelling and at times utterly beautiful. It is a game of forgetting who you really are. As Alan Watts says, 'God also likes to play hide-and-seek, but because there is nothing outside God, he has no one but himself to play with.'

To be in the world and not be consumed by it, you need to affirm the Light as your true nature. Nothing affirms this more than by enjoying the playfulness of the play of life itself, which is, after all, why you are here.

18

The Mystery of Prayer

The heart has its reasons which reason knows nothing of…
Blaise Pascal

Whichever way you look at it, prayer is a mystery, and you cannot get your head around mystery; you can only get your heart around it.

Next to your bed you have a very treasured picture of an old man with a beard, wearing nothing but a loin cloth. His eyes shine like diamonds in the sun, and his loving smile draws you deeper and deeper into his loving presence. It is here, whilst looking into his grace-bestowing gaze, that the person you think yourself to be just melts away. His eyes transmit something to you that is impossible to convey through words. You are drawn ever deeper into these beautiful eyes that reflect back to you your true, timeless and unchanging nature. This man's name is Bhagavan Ramana Maharshi, the sage of Arunachala, and one glance at his picture is worth a thousand prayers.

Your soul's journey home is to truly embody the statement made by Hanuman to Ram in the Hindu epic 'Ramayana', 'When I do not know who I am, I serve You and when I do know who I am, You and I are One.' This statement says so much to you with respect to prayer, devotion and intimacy with the divine. It embodies the two approaches commonly reflected in many religious traditions, one being the path of prayer and surrender, the other being the pathless path of direct experience. For you, it has never been a case of following either one approach or the other, for you are equally at home within your intuitive mind as you are with your heart.

You see prayer as a movement outwards as well as inwards. Simply being still and dwelling in the present moment is, in itself, a movement into prayer. However, the experience of prayer is really hard to convey through words or concepts. Having the simplest faith is the most beautiful thing in the world to you, and when your life is lived through this faith, then everything you do becomes an act of worship and adoration.

Prayer for you is a doorway into the oneness that permeates everything. This is the most sublime of all mysteries.

19

'Being' in Uncertainty

The Greater the Certainty, the Less the Understanding.

Anonymous

It is often hard to admit doubt with respect to your faith, as it can often leave you feeling in an anxious state of being uncertain. Consequently, you can at times find it hard to be completely honest with yourself and simply 'be' in the uncertainty of doubt.

Time and time again you learn that where there is resistance within you, there remains conflict and disharmony. Allowing things to be as they are simply affirms the lessons that you need to learn in order to wake up to who you are. So easy it is to busy away the discomfort associated with doubt. Have faith in your doubting that it will lead to a movement into greater depth of awareness.

In *A Field Guide to Getting Lost*, the American writer, Rebecca Solnit, made a perceptive observation. She said, 'To be lost is to be fully present, and to be fully present is to be capable of being in uncertainty and mystery.'

In the spiritual life, there remains a taboo amongst many that doubt is in some way a hindrance or unacceptable. This attitude can often result in you hiding away your feelings, being inadequate or feeling a failure, believing that in some way they are wrong.

Faith, like an open hand, has a releasing and letting go quality, in contrast to belief, which, like a closed fist, can only contain and ultimately constrict. When you are able to cry out your anguish and be honest about doubt, there is often a letting go that brings harmony and freedom. Experience has shown you that if you can be honest with yourself and allow doubt a place in your life, this can lead to infinite creativity where new insight can be found.

Being with uncertainty is an invitation to go deeper into the mystery of who you really are.

20

Waiting in the Light

*For what gave us our identity was not a common set of beliefs,
but a common practice: waiting in silence – in the light.*

Rex Ambler

Waiting in the Light is a way of seeing beyond your
habitual and finite way of perceiving.

You have discovered that Quakers place enormous
importance on this 'waiting' in all areas of their lives,
corporately and personally. Discernment and decision-
making would be empty and without real meaning if they
were not disciplined in this Light-filled waiting.

However, being on the autism spectrum, you are
seriously challenged by organising, prioritising and
impulsivity. Consequently, you see 'waiting in the Light'
as a dynamic holding back from trying to work everything
out with your habitual mind. It is such a gift to get out of
your mind and into the Light.

You use the term 'Light' interchangeably with
'awareness' and 'God' or simply 'consciousness'. It is
of little importance what you call it; however, the word
'Light' seems such a simple and universal metaphor for
the spiritual life.

'The light', said George Fox, 'is that by which ye come
to see.' He went on to say, 'When the light discloses and
reveals things to you, things that tempt you, confuse you,
don't go on looking at them, but look at the light that
has made you aware of them.' This advice you find most

valuable, as the drama of being in the world can at times be so compelling and overwhelming.

Waiting or pausing takes enormous skill and practice. However, it is a skill that for you has become an essential way of being in the world without being so overwhelmed by it. Viktor Frankl, the Austrian psychiatrist and Holocaust survivor, went even further when he famously said, 'Between stimulus and response there is a space. In that space is our power to choose our response. In our response lies our growth and our freedom.'

Waiting in the Light enables you to create a space for grace.

21

Whisper 'Yes'

> *... All you ever longed for is*
> *before you in this moment*
> *if you dare draw in a*
> *breath and whisper 'Yes.'*
>
> Danna Faulds, from her poem 'White Dove'

Whilst it is true that you are a person on the autism spectrum, your true identity is the light of loving awareness that shines within you.

Being on the autism spectrum, together with all the dramas of your past, is simply part of a script for your awakening in this life. Your challenge is to meet all that comes your way with presence, and in so doing your life becomes nothing other than a pilgrimage into the very heart of being human.

However, there are times when you find it just too overwhelming to stay present with the waves of discomfort that flow through your being. In such times, you whisper with loving tenderness, 'Yes' or 'I consent'. This can often soften your resistance and dampen down the hyperactivity in your nervous system.

In giving your 'Yes' to the many experiences that you would habitually push away, you make that movement from your small and contracted sense of self, to that deeper part of you that is your true nature. It takes courage to see things as they are and not merely as you would wish them to be. In being present to life in such a way, you find you are able to create a more spacious awareness around people, places and things that would otherwise overwhelm you.

In so doing you slowly wake up to the truth that what you have always longed for is right in front of you, right here, right now. The verse above from Danna Faulds' evocative poem 'White Dove' is a beautiful reminder of this.

All *you* need to do is draw in a breath and whisper 'Yes.'

22

The Play of Darkness and Light

If you bring forth what is within you, what you bring forth will save you. If you do not bring forth what is within you, what you do not bring forth will destroy you.

Gospel of Thomas

You remember the day as if it was yesterday, and that first look in his eyes, a look that said,

'You are special.'

No words can ever come close in conveying the deep sadness that had led to that fateful day and what followed afterwards, when, as a 14-year-old boy, accompanied by your parents, you found yourself in the consulting room of one of the world's eminent child psychiatrists. The warmth emanating from this man towards you was as intense as it was overwhelming, leaving you feeling truly alive. The problem was...he felt exactly the same.

A childhood of unrelenting emotional neglect had led you into the care of this man the world would call a paedophile, yet you would call a special friend who never really was. You fell completely under his spell and influence whilst you were in his care, both in hospital and after you were discharged. You believed that his warmth towards you would save you from the insanity caused by a childhood spent in deep freeze.

As is true in cases of sexual abuse, this relationship was based purely on exploitation, secrecy and lies. In this respect it was no different from any other relationship that you had formed up to that point. Yet like all painful experiences in your life, what ultimately hurt the most was not the acts of cruelty themselves, but the web of secrecy that surrounded such a cruel violation of boundaries.

To break free you had to reclaim your anger, for anger was the only energy that could pierce the veil of shame surrounding the sexual abuse that weighed so heavily upon your heart. Yet such anger terrified you. Where could you go to scream that loudly and not be locked up? Whom could you trust to help you? Who would really believe you anyway? After all, the key player in your story was a highly respected pillar of society.

When you did break free, what followed was decades of highly skilled spiritual and psychological support from which eventually an authentic and integrated spirituality slowly emerged. In laying bare the unbearable agony from a shattered self, and the overwhelming grief that came from holding it all to the Light, you came to reconcile the seemingly irreconcilable elements within your psyche. In diving deep into your own darkness, you came to see the collective darkness of humanity and how good and evil reside in us all.

'That which we do not bring to consciousness', says Carl Jung, 'appears in our lives as fate.'

You do not condone the awful things that happened to you, nor do you spiritualise away the enormity of pain and anguish. Over time you learned to hold deeply and tenderly the whole human drama of it all, including a grief so dark and terrifying that you feared you would never survive. Yet from out of the fiery darkness of such grief you did emerge, no longer a prisoner of the hurt, for you were set free – free to forgive, not only yourself, but also the doctor.

At first you had resisted this letting go of anger, feeling that it was justified and still necessary. However, the game had changed, for you had glimpsed a view of another dimension. Here there was no such thing as paedophile or victim, or even self and other; as Krishna said in the *Bhagavad Gita*:

> He that slays or he that is slain, if he thinks there is a slayer or a slain, knows not me.

23

Dancing with Fear

Our deepest fears are like dragons guarding our deepest treasure.

Rainer Maria Rilke

Fear has brought you to your knees more than anything else, and it is for this very reason that fear has become a most valuable dancing partner in your awakening to truth. This is echoed in the words of the Tibetan Buddhist, Pema Chödrön, 'Fear is a natural reaction to moving closer to the truth.'

After many years of talking, writing and acting out your fears, the time has now come to breathe through them and allow them to all fall away into the very silence from which they came. When you can allow fear, which often has its roots in past experiences, to float in and out of your consciousness with no clinging or judgement, you create a spacious awareness around the melodrama of your life. This not only takes practice, contemplative practice, it also takes enormous courage, patience and persistence.

This process is not to be confused with the contracted or fearful holding back connected with disassociation. Whereas in the past you held back in terror and complete darkness, today your holding back is more within the spacious loving light of awareness itself.

Whilst many people seek spirituality to reassure themselves about death and dying, you see spirituality as all about 'being' here now. Beliefs and belief systems are merely part of the mind, so as the mind ceases to function, so, too, will your beliefs. You have found that clinging to belief when in the grip of fear only conceals and prolongs your suffering. Belief always needs to 'hold on', whilst having faith in what *is* fosters an unreserved opening of the mind to the truth.

Your identity is not that of a survivor, but a victor! To be a survivor means to be defined by your past to some extent or other. To be a victor means to be free of the identification with your past and to dwell in the timeless present. It is here that you will find the deepest treasure.

24

Divine Play of Father and Son

*There was never a time when you and I did not exist,
...nor will there come a time when we will cease to be.*

Bhagavad Gita

The Sanskrit word 'guru' literally means 'the one who dispels the darkness of ignorance'. In so many ways your son has been the greatest of gurus to you.

The love, both given and received, which continuously flows between you and your son, takes you out from your place of darkness, where until now you have been under the illusion that you are somehow separate from humanity and the world. In so doing your son becomes a mirror that reflects back to you your true nature.

You continue to awaken through this love that flows between you both, love which, like a true guru, is ever present within, regardless of how far away physically you are from each other. He is always there, living and breathing within your heart. Often you ask yourself, 'Who is teaching whom here?'

'Love is essentially self-communicative;' says the Indian spiritual teacher Meher Baba, 'those who do not have it catch it from those who have it.' Here you enter into a most sublime paradox, that the love that has been an agent in your awakening is not actually coming from your son but through him. Understanding this, and seeing this in play, enables you, through your loving role as a parent, to move from your role into your soul, within the drama of everyday life.

You are not defined by your neurodiversity, or by the traumas of your past. You are defined by the love that flows between you and your son. Such a love evokes in you the innate love that has always been in you, ever reminding you of the deeper reality – that you and your son are simply the Light dressed up in playing the divine game of father and son.

25

Going Underground

The joy may be in the journey, yet the true destination is within.

Christopher Goodchild

The London Underground has a very special place in your life.

Your childhood home was situated beside the Metropolitan Line, and the rattling and whistling sounds the trains made as they passed by the end of your garden were music to your ears. On summer nights the blackbirds would sing their melancholy song, which would mingle in the air, harmonising with the sounds of the trains as if playing a duet. The soothing metronome effect made by the rhythmic sound of the wheels on the tracks would offer you comfort, although at the same time it evoked a great longing within you, a longing to be anywhere but where you were. How you ached to jump aboard this snaking train that could transport you away from the dullness of the suburbs into the capital where everything would be alive and vibrant.

Today you are very happy to be where you are, in the centre of London, and the London Underground still features largely in your life. You travel the tube, not because it takes you anywhere – though clearly that is one purpose – but the combination of movement and visual stimulus also offers you the perfect conditions to write. It amuses you to know that, in some languages, the words for 'travelling' and 'thinking' are identical.

Whilst it is true that being in such close proximity to others can be overwhelming, the total absorption in your writing anchors you within another dimension altogether. This sense of being together on a human journey whilst travelling through the darkness is profoundly moving for you.

Finding such a mystical experience such as this in an everyday situation can often reduce you to tears. On an average day you will spend at least two hours travelling the London Underground system. Over the course of the year, this would amount to one entire month spent deep down underneath the clay of London. It is time well spent.

Often your thoughts turn with great affection to the many Londoners who took shelter in tube stations during the Second World War. Whilst Londoners during the blitz sought refuge there from the bombs falling from the sky, you take refuge there from London's overcrowded streets, where no public seats can ever be found, and the weather in winter can be cold and inhospitable. It is a thrill to escape from the sensory mayhem and harshness above ground, by sitting on a warm seat in a quiet spot right at the end of a deserted platform in Leicester Square tube station. It is here you can stop, relax and enjoy your packed lunch with hardly anyone around. Often, when you have finished your meal, you make your gratitude known by offering a little smile to the CCTV camera, in a similar manner in which a person in a restaurant might express thanks to a waiter after leaving a tip.

You do not see yourself as a passenger, you see yourself as a traveller, and whilst the joy may be in the journey, as Rilke pointed out, 'The only journey is the one within.'

26

Dropping Your Anchor

When there is silence
One finds peace.
When there is silence
One finds the anchor of the universe within himself.

Lao Tzu

Space is as precious to you as your in-breath and out-breath. This is true whether this space is a pause between your thoughts and your response, or a moment of sensory calm found amidst the swirling movement and drama of life in London. Space enables you to be in the world and not be so overwhelmed by it. Space also allows you to come home to who you really are, enabling you to then engage with the world from a deeper place within, creating a space for grace.

You are a wanderer. Unable to write at home where you feel the walls hem you in and constrict you, you spend your days walking around London's streets, walkways, alleys and heaths. Here you can breathe, the sky is your natural ceiling and the air on your face sets in motion a movement within you whereby you can write unimpeded and free. You draw endless inspiration from the rich diversity and drama of the capital. People often say to you, 'How can you, a person on the autism spectrum, tolerate all the unrelenting noise and mayhem in the capital?' Your answer often falls upon deaf ears, for whilst on one level London can be an enormously challenging sensory environment for you, on another level it is also a continuously unfolding love affair. You find music in its noise and poetry in its mayhem.

Like any wanderer, you need to find a place to rest, to gather yourself, allowing your thoughts to drop mindfully into place. It is for this reason that you take refuge in any one of the little cluster of Catholic churches that are scattered around the centre of London's West End. Often completely alone, you can now observe your breathing, bringing your attention to your entire in-breath and out-breath. Then, slowly, you begin to write. You write until the cleaner starts their shift. When the cleaning of the candles, with its clattering and scraping, finally gets under way, you get on your way to the church round the corner, until the candle scrapers come out there too. Then you simply return to where you started. This is how you write.

In many ways the drama of London life, combined with the sensory havens of these little churches, offers you the ideal stimulus and rest that enables you to write. You are no longer a practising Catholic, yet the church continues to open its doors to you, enabling you to drop anchor within yourself and to help meet your needs in a way which you could never really have imagined.

27

Laughter as a Doorway

As soon as you have made a thought, laugh at it.

Lao Tzu

Like many people with high-functioning autism, you have a very imaginative and expansive sense of humour. Laughter brings you endless fun as well as helping you to put spacious awareness around afflicting thoughts, feelings and situations. Laughter also softens the edges of your natural propensity for intensity, which helps you to live more creatively.

Whilst those closest to you delight in your quirky wordplay and idiosyncratic ways, your sense of humour can also be your way of responding to a world that is unpredictable and overwhelming. At times, when in the company of other people, you use humour to manage emotionally charged situations. Often this is expressed by chuckling inwardly to yourself, and creating imaginative scenarios that amuse you. This creates distance, in the same way as looking away and avoiding eye contact with a person who is flooding you or demanding your attention.

It is an endless source of amusement to create humour around the shadow side of your nature too. For you the shadow and humour are complementary elements that work together in taking you deeper into your divine nature. Laughter does this by helping to bring into awareness those parts of yourself that you had previously refused to acknowledge, such as your autism. This enables you to make peace with, and what is more, to laugh at, those things you were previously unable to accept. Moreover, laughter can hold the power to dislodge your attachment to the masks you wear in daily life. This is so elegantly captured in the poem 'Eternity' by William Blake:

He who binds to himself a joy
Does the winged life destroy;
But he who kisses the joy as it flies
Lives in eternity's sun rise.

Laughter and spirituality go hand in hand for you. Like ecstatic spiritual experiences, laughter can take you away from trying to control everything or work everything out in your head, enabling you to drop into your heart. There is a parallel here with the early Quakers and Shakers, who would tremble and shake before God. Therefore you continually delight in your capacity to laugh at yourself, religion and the human condition.

Laughter offers you a doorway into a spiritual dimension. The words of the Swiss theologian Karl Barth resonate deeply within you when he says, 'Laughter is the closest thing to the grace of God.'

28

Entrusting Yourself
to the Waves

Drift east and west, come and go, entrusting yourself to the waves.

Ryokan

Like many people on the autism spectrum, your mind can seem as though it has very little filtering. You are unable to screen out extraneous sounds, feelings and thoughts that often seem to crash into you like waves upon a turbulent sensory ocean.

Your experience of being flooded by stimulation can often leave you feeling very distressed and overwhelmed. In such times memories of the past where you have been incapacitated by fear or desperation come flooding into your mind, bringing you to the verge of panic. When this happens, you have found it invaluable to remember that whilst the distress is very real, the beliefs attached to such painful experiences are often without any foundation in the present. It has merely triggered a response that is still imprinted in your nervous system from early trauma. What is real is not necessarily what is true, however much your frantically beating heart might suggest otherwise.

Often it can feel as though you are torn between two patterns of reactivity – pushing away fear or getting tangled up in it. Entrusting yourself to the waves means witnessing the waves of thoughts and memories, whilst at the same time holding intimately this fear of being overwhelmed, as you would hold with tenderness and compassion a fearful sparrow that has dropped out of the sky and into the palm of your hand.

This creates the conditions whereby you can soften and discharge the residue of early trauma associated with being powerless and out of control. If you can remain faithful to this contemplative practice in such times, a deeper wisdom can emerge. This is reflected in the enlightened statement from Meister Eckhart, 'What used to be a hindrance now helps you most.'

Through the daily practice of surrendering into the midst of life you can make that authentic movement from what feels real into what is true.

29

The Shadowlands

Truly, it is in the darkness that one finds the light, so when we are in sorrow, then this light is nearest of all to us.

Meister Eckhart

Your small contracted sense of self does not want to go there, but if you truly wish to be free, you have no real choice but to enter into the shadowlands of your being and befriend this 'other' half of you. To not do so would simply hold you back from progressing in the spiritual life.

It matters not what you call this part of you that you have unconsciously deemed either intolerable or unacceptable. What matters is that you listen to its calling within you and reach out across this mysterious divide and make friends with the deepest and darkest depths of your psyche. 'It is not by looking into the light that we become luminous,' said Jung, 'but by plunging into the darkness. However, this is often unpleasant work, and therefore not very popular.'

As a child with autism you were told daily by your parents that you were odd, peculiar, strange and mad. This experience was traumatic. To survive you had to force down all the rejection and feelings associated with such enormous psychological wounding. Out of this horror a mask of 'normality' was created in you unknowingly. Its purpose was to simply keep you sane, and to protect you from the overwhelming despair you felt in your heart. Also it was to your advantage to conceal your natural way of being, preventing any further humiliating abuse.

You survived your childhood. However, to truly live your life as an adult you had to allow your mask of normality to fall. Intense suffering was eventually to lead you to the formal diagnosis of being on the autism spectrum. With this new understanding and insight, alongside the support of skilled spiritual directors and psychologists, you slowly entered into the shadowlands of your being. Through this process you made friends with what you had been conditioned to believe was unacceptable. Your autism.

Befriending your shadow came at a cost. You lost your over-attachment to the person you thought yourself to be and were confronted with the enormous suffering that you had been previously insulated from. Such disorientation and grief was overwhelming and changed you at a very deep level.

Being completely honest with yourself is the deepest spiritual practice you can undertake. Until this is wholeheartedly embraced, your spiritual life will always rest to some extent or other upon unsound psychological foundations.

30

A Wounded Tree Still Blossoms

How we squander our hours of pain. How we gaze beyond them into the bitter duration to see if they have an end. Though they are really our winter-enduring foliage, our dark evergreen, one season in our inner year.

Rainer Maria Rilke

Walking through the woods it never ceases to amaze you how extraordinary some of the old trees are. Nothing captures your imagination quite so much as the beautifully ornate and intricate roots and limbs of some of the trees there. Many of these have gained their unusual beauty by having to adapt to survive due to injury. Their uniqueness comes not from the original injury, but from the essential nature inherent within the tree itself that the trauma dramatically drew out.

In so many ways these beautiful trees capture your heart, and reflect back to you your own true and essential nature, as well as your courageous human journey lived out here on earth, the very same earth that these beautiful trees are rooted in.

Soon after your formal diagnosis with high-functioning autism, you embarked upon an unrelenting process of enquiry, presenting yourself, with such curiosity and persistence, to endless specialists in the areas of psychology and autism in search of answers. Your journey took you from running away from suffering, to then becoming over-identified with it. Like a hamster on a wheel, you were merely changing direction yet still running. It took you falling off the wheel completely, through depression, to wake up to the fact that whilst you were continuing to run, you were still being claimed by your past to some extent or other.

Today you have put into a good enough retirement place the compartmentalising and analysis of why you are the way you are, and as a result you have found a peace that had forever evaded you.

Whilst there remains a residue of trauma within you, you have learned to hold this wound tenderly and with skilful loving awareness. So much so that today you are strong enough to embrace what was too overwhelming in the past to even bring to awareness. You no longer push away your past, nor do you cling to it. Your story has become His-story.

Walking through the woods you feel a deep sense of belonging. You have come to see that the trees have their stories too, and that they hold the joy as well as the sadness of humanity.

Of all the trees in the woods, it is those that have been shaped by adversity that touch you most deeply. Under the stars, in the cool breeze of a dark summer night, they whisper to you… 'A wounded tree still blossoms.'

31

Eating Poppies with the Dead

Only he who has eaten
poppies with the dead will not lose ever again
the gentlest chord.
Though the image upon the pool
often grows dim:
Know and be still.

Rainer Maria Rilke

'You're strange!' 'Odd!' 'Mad!' 'Peculiar!' These were the words that would be thrown at you every day as a child by people who should have known different. Their words spat out like daggers into your heart.

It seemed that as soon as you were able to walk you were put down for being different – unable to give eye contact comfortably, lining up objects obsessively around the home, and unable to conceal all your unusual behaviours which were seen as unacceptable. Little was known about high-functioning autism and developmental trauma when you were growing up. By the time you reached the age of 15, you lost all desire to live and were consequently committed to a psychiatric hospital. After a year of being admitted you gave up all hope of ever integrating into 'normal' society.

The horror of slipping into such an abyss at such a vulnerable age was cataclysmic. Many hours you spent walking through the crumbling walkways of that Victorian asylum, witnessing emaciated bodies shuffling along like ghosts, with minds so tortured and brutalised by stories that were most likely unspeakable, and buried under an avalanche of psychiatric medications.

This experience of such intense human suffering was so overwhelming that your habitual way of seeing reality was totally shattered. It was here that it seemed you crossed the great divide which separated you from 'others', for you simply felt inseparably connected, through suffering, to humanity. This experience moved you from your pain to *the* pain of humanity. It was as though your empathic pathways, which up to that point had seemed blocked, became blown open to embrace the suffering of the world.

You saw the human condition so consumed by suffering and despair, and yet from out of this darkness came a light that, deep inside, you knew could never be extinguished, the Light of your true and timeless nature.

The American poet Rashani Réa captures beautifully this inner strength born out of adversity in her stunning poem, 'The Unbroken'.

*There is a brokenness
out of which comes the unbroken,
a shatteredness
out of which blooms the unshatterable.
There is a sorrow
beyond all grief which leads to joy
and a fragility
out of whose depths emerges strength...*

You shall never forget those lost and vulnerable people whom you met in the asylum. Many were unlikely to have ever left. Certainly, they have never left you. They hold a very special place in your heart.

32

The Ocean and the Waves

The heart is nothing but the sea of light...

Rumi

The ocean and the waves cannot be separated. The ocean for you is a wonderful metaphor for your true nature, whilst the waves convey the drama of your human incarnation – the play of the ultimate and the relative.

Whilst the ocean and the waves are one, the waves play the game of trying to convince you otherwise. Therefore, it is your practice to be awake to the deeper reality of the ocean, so that even in the most overwhelming circumstances you can affirm that part of you which is free. 'When we know that we are the ocean,' says Sri Nisargadatta, 'we cease to be fearful of the waves.'

The play of duality is compelling. In the Hindu tradition, it is referred to as 'Leela', the cosmic dance of form or divine sport. Applying this principle to the ocean and the waves, you can see yourself as simply the oneness playing the divine game of being the many.

You still have a part to play out within the game of duality for many reasons. Who would really want to be a spoilsport and wake up too soon and miss the fun? You have come to see that in loving the game of duality, you affirm and honour the reason you are here in the first place. After all, duality is all part of the oneness that permeates everything anyway. You have no desire to play the game of being anyone other than who you are – being human *and* divine at the same time.

There are not many people in the world who are totally free from identifying with the waves and drama of the world. People like Jesus, Buddha and Ramana Maharshi do not come that often, and when they do, most of us are completely unprepared for what they have to say, or how to live out their teaching.

The ocean and the waves are one and you are already this ocean of oneness. In time you will see this. Be this.

33

The Mountain of Truth

My convictions led me to adhere to the sufficiency of the light within us, resting on truth as authority, rather than 'taking authority for truth'.

Lucretia Mott

Whilst you love the game of using words and delight in linguistic playfulness, at the end of the day, words are not something you get too attached to in your journeying up the mountain of truth. As Shakespeare pointed out, 'a rose By any other name would smell as sweet'.

With respect to ultimate truth, you find the image of a mountain most helpful. On one side, you have the spiritual path up the mountain, whilst on the other side is the path of objective reasoning and science. Both paths speak to different sides of your nature; they are simply different expressions of the same reality. You walk more naturally up the spiritual side of the mountain, but this is only because you have a more poetic sensibility and can only fully grasp concepts and ideas through your intuitive mind. However, you also have a passion for science and a deep respect for objective reasoning. Even though this might be considered unusual, in this you are not alone. After all, Albert Einstein, whom many believe was on the autism spectrum, clearly had the capacity to hold both the mystical and the rational in dynamic balance. 'I want to know how God created the world,' he said, 'I am not interested in this or that phenomenon, in the spectrum of this or that element; I want to know his thoughts; the rest are details.'

This balance of left and right hemispheres, this coming together of the intuitive mind and objective reasoning, excites you enormously. Too easy it is to fall prey to 'either/or' thinking, for such a mindset can stifle your creativity and squeeze your imagination. It is for this reason that you have found the Indian philosophy of Advaita Vedanta a wonderfully unifying and insightful guide to scaling internally the mountain of truth.

Spirituality for you is all about understanding the meaning of your existence. It seeks a unified language and yet can often seem a much less concrete and more meandering path to tread. Science, on the other hand, has a more precise, 'just so', approach, which appeals to your autistic brain. However, it makes no sense to you that one path should be lacking the key aspects of the other. They are complementary to each other, like yin and yang.

What seems clear to you is that the finite mind can never comprehend the infinite, and that blind adherence to rules, dogma and beliefs, regardless of which path you tread, are no real substitute for having an open heart, curiosity and a spirit of true adventure.

34

The Gift of Not Knowing

Not knowing when the dawn will come I open every door.

Emily Dickinson

Letting go of trying to work everything out in your head can lead you directly into the most sublime mystery of all. Your heart. Your true Self. To open yourself to this mystery, you will often have to pass through the discomfort of the rational mind simply 'not knowing'.

What at first might seem like an impending breakdown can easily become a profound breakthrough. This is beautifully conveyed in 'The Real Work' by Wendell Berry:

> It may be that when we no longer know what to do we have come to our real work, and that when we no longer know which way to go we have begun our real journey. The mind that is not baffled is not employed. The impeded stream is the one that sings.

The emotional distress that often accompanies losing your direction in life cannot be glamorised nor underestimated, when you are unable to come up with a rational solution to your predicament. However, it is true to say that one of the greatest gifts you have received in this life is the gift of desperation directly linked to the rational mind not coming up trumps.

In many ways 'being' in uncertainty and mystery is a necessary rite of passage you must go through in order to enter into the heart of what it means to be most alive. As a writer you see it as a vocational calling for you to invite the unfamiliar. In living your life in this way you surrender into something greater, your perceptions are stretched, as is your imagination – pushing the boundaries of what is unknown and unforeseen.

The breakthrough experience, whereby you move from lost to found, is exhilarating. The attachment to the small self is loosened, and an infinitely larger, more expansive Self is glimpsed. It is here, in these glimpses that a startling new landscape, or perhaps a radically new way of seeing, is opened up within you. Here the words of Jesus come to mind, 'For those who want to save their life will lose it, and those who lose their life for my sake will find it.'

To embrace the gift of not knowing is to embark on one of the greatest adventures, and one that if fully entered into will change your life forever.

35

The Seeker

Jesus said, 'Let him who seeks continue seeking until he finds. When he finds, he will become troubled. When he becomes troubled, he will be astonished...'

Gospel of Thomas

Although being a seeker is part of why you are here, the aim of all seeking is ultimately to give up the duality of being the 'seeker' and to merge into the oneness that permeates everything.

One of the paradoxes of the spiritual life is that the more you become aware, the more you realise how unaware you are. However, when you can accept this with an open heart and simply laugh into the whole drama of your imperfections, a deeper reality unfolds within you. This deeper reality has nothing to do with getting anywhere or doing anything, for there is no 'where' you really need to go, and no 'thing' you really need to do.

Seeking continues until you are ready to give up seeking, and it has been your experience that this is impossible until you realise, in the depth of your heart, that you are already what you seek, and that there is no separation between you and absolutely everyone and everything else. Who you really are exists without your thinking mind, however much your thinking mind would have you believe otherwise.

Intense and overwhelming suffering have in the past become like portals that offered you a glimpse into another dimension. It was as though you got stuck in a particular way of thinking until something disturbing knocked you sideways and jolted you into a new way of seeing things.

It has been the grieving process associated with each respective loss that often takes you to the next level of awareness. A part of you, your ego, would rather die than face the level of distress that overwhelming grief would cause you. This is where it gets interesting, because with each sorrow grieved the person you have believed yourself to be dies little by little until the 'you' that you believed yourself to be ceases to exist.

Seen in this way suffering can become like a fire of purification that takes you to the point of no return. Your life has been shaped by such suffering. 'Are you willing to be sponged out,' says D.H. Lawrence, 'erased, cancelled, made nothing? Are you willing to be made nothing, dipped into oblivion? If not, you will never really change.'

Faced with this reality, who but a madman or someone mad in pursuit of truth would dare embark upon such an undertaking?

36

The Sacred Heart of Jesus

When you make the two one, and when
*   you make the inner as the outer*
and the outer as the inner...
then you shall enter [the kingdom].

Gospel of Thomas

You have always felt deeply drawn to the Sacred Heart of
Jesus.

For many years now you have contemplated this image
in churches and through works of art. Often this devotional
image portrays Jesus pointing to his heart, as though he
is saying that this (the heart) *is* the kingdom, and that this
mysterious space is within you and all around you.

Whilst your love for Jesus has never waned, what have
waned for you are the dogma and the belief systems that
have woven themselves around him. Like many Quakers,
you ache for the truth that Jesus spoke about, rather than
what that truth has been so conveniently wrapped up in.
The ethical and moral dimension of Jesus's teaching is
clear to be seen. However, for you he is so much more,
for he embodies 'being love', and his most fundamental
message is to take this 'being love' out into the world.
To you this is the kingdom that is within you and all
around you.

Jesus's teachings and parables wake you up to this
'kingdom within' by jolting you out of your conditioned
mind. This is no easy undertaking, as the beliefs that have
supported and protected you in the past are now seen
as obstacles to you progressing in your journey to true
enlightenment. The love you feel for Jesus evokes such
strong devotion, and it is through such devotion that the
person you believe yourself to be becomes smaller and
smaller. So small, that at times you slip through the chains
that bind you to your small contracted sense of self. It is
here that you are reminded of the words of Saint Paul,
when he said, 'I have been crucified with Christ...and it
is no longer I who live, but it is Christ who lives in me.'

There will always be mystery surrounding devotional
practice that the rational mind can never come close to
understanding. Once you can accept this and allow your
heart to lead, you will be set free. Through the imagery of
the Sacred Heart, Jesus is pointing to the only place where

the real answers can be found – the heart – and the only way they can be experienced – through love.

This takes faith, and faith for you is most true when it is most simple and you are able to put your whole life behind it. Then faith becomes a doorway into the divine. All this moves within you as you gaze into the image of the Sacred Heart of Jesus.

37

The Infinite Sky Within

...its repetition will eventually be fruitful – like a seed fallen on the roof of a deserted house which crumbles over decades, finally enabling the germinated seed to take root...

Sri Ramakrishna

Chanting offers you a doorway into a deeper dimension, taking you from your small contracted sense of self into something infinitely more expansive.

If entered into with an open heart, the repetition of a holy name can become like a river of devotion that carries you through your day. Just as the endless flowing of a river slowly erodes rock, the repetition of a mantra can reshape your interior landscape.

You have a formal practice of chanting in the mornings and the evenings and rarely does a day pass without you listening to devotional chanting of some kind or other. However, chanting has the most powerful effect when you practise it throughout the day, particularly when you find yourself in large crowds of people.

You love chanting in the London Underground, as this not only manages the distress of being bombarded with such frenetic energy, but it can also transform the experience for you from a place of disconnection to a web of connectivity. The rhythm, repetition and vibration that you experience when chanting a mantra is soothing for your nervous system and brings great relief when you are overwhelmed. It is as though your tightly contracted body softens and releases, and even more importantly, so does your perception of those all around you.

On this deeper level, chanting for you holds the key to unlocking the inner eye of your heart, allowing you to see the Light behind the myriad of masks and roles that the people around you assume in everyday life, be they jarringly loud, suited and proud or ragged and defeated. As it says in the *Bhagavad Gita*, 'For those who see me everywhere and see all things in me, I am never lost, nor are they ever lost to me.'

You do not need to try to be aware, for you *are* loving awareness itself, but you do need a practice that wakes you up to this reality throughout the drama of your daily life. Chanting is such a practice. The silent singing of a mantra does not so much remove obstacles that stand in your way, but enables you to use these very 'obstacles' as a means of falling into the flow of grace. Then you can see that everyone and everything is simply a part of the oneness that permeates everything – buskers on the Underground, drivers hooting on the road, and birds singing in the air around. All sing as one.

Whilst it is commonplace for people to sing, hum and whistle through the day, you simply chant. Wherever you go you chant silently under your breath, and in so doing you free fall into the infinite sky within.

38

'Being' En Route

Wisdom consists in doing the next thing you have to do, doing it with your whole heart, and finding delight in doing it.

Meister Eckhart

When you were younger, you loved taking on the world. Today you enjoy letting it all pass you by.

Life for you is no longer about getting anywhere fast. It is about being here now and giving your full attention to what is right in front of you. Drawing from this well of mindfulness throughout your day you call 'being' en route.

The temptation is often to rush things and get them out of the way in order to have quiet time.

The irony in living like this is that you never really arrive at all, for when you eventually stop, your time is simply spent catching up with yourself at the expense of 'being' in your quiet time.

So easy it is to put the meditative hat on or off in accordance with the endless drama that is always there within and all around you. However, your calling to live the contemplative life more authentically challenges you to overcome this inconsistency. Whilst you cannot stop the endless thoughts that forever flow through your awareness, you can have a very different relationship with them.

One of the many ways in which you practice being in the present moment is to name and label intrusive thoughts and feelings that can often clamour for your attention. In so doing you discharge the stuck energy and dis-ease that inevitably comes through unconsciously attempting to busy away or get tangled up in the drama. When there is fear you bow internally and say to yourself, 'Fear, fear.' When there is sadness you say, 'Sadness, sadness.'

However, the fact remains that you are a very imperfect practitioner, and at the end of the day fear and sadness remain. When this becomes apparent, you stop. You put your hand on your heart and affirm it saying, 'Okay, I see you. Breathing in, I am aware of sadness and fear; breathing out, I smile lovingly into sadness and fear.' This mindfulness approach, inspired by the Vietnamese Zen master Thich Nhat Hanh, is such a wonderful way of soothing and calming your agitation.

Walking, too, is a beautiful way of coming back to your Self. Whenever you feel overwhelmed or embroiled in intrusive thoughts or uncomfortable feelings, you simply name the thought, and turn your attention to the rhythm of your breathing. As you walk, the swinging of your arms either side like pendulums is so soothing and reassuring. This so beautifully embodies 'being' en route.

Sometimes you are just not able to throw the mindfulness spanner into the works, to stop the pattern of reactivity. Here you can reach a place of surrender and acceptance whereby grace can then come through and transform you.

'Being' en route is all about living life sacramentally and waking up from out of the dreamlike state in which you would otherwise habitually live your life.

39

Autism... It's Not What You Think

He who sees the infinite in all things, sees God.
He who sees the Ratio only sees himself only.

William Blake

Your mind is not so much conscious, but an instrument of consciousness. You have little interest in believing theories about how your mind works, but every interest in consciousness itself, and in observing it and learning from what you experience.

Autism is for you a way of being, and as such can never adequately be conveyed through theories, concepts or analysis. 'I didn't arrive', said Albert Einstein, 'at my understanding of the fundamental laws of the universe through my rational mind.' And you know exactly where he was coming from.

Your early experience of the educational system was daunting. It placed emphasis on teaching what to think over how to think, and on rewarding those with good memories at the expense of good ideas. Such a system can contribute to a society lacking imagination and insight into the subtleties of humanity. This lack of insight is there to be seen in the area of autism, where many specialists inevitably succumb to a 'this is the way that it is' mindset, when 'it' is often totally at odds with your own experience of being on the autism spectrum.

Autism is for you a way of perceiving reality in a particular way. Oscar Wilde enters into this wonderfully when he says, 'The final mystery is oneself. When one has weighed the sun in the balance, and measured the steps of the moon, and mapped out the seven heavens star by star, there still remains oneself. Who can calculate the orbit of his own soul?'

People on the autism spectrum offer a unique and rich dimension to humanity as a whole, which is not just limited to the areas of science, maths, information technology and engineering. For it is equally true to say that amongst people on the spectrum there are numerous contemplatives, many of whom you have met yourself. In the areas of poetry and literature too, there is a very long list of writers who were most likely on the spectrum, people like Emily Dickinson, Lewis Carroll and Hans Christian Andersen. Also, in the area of philosophy there are people like Henry Thoreau, Bertrand Russell and Ludwig Wittgenstein, to name just a few. Such diversity can never be confined to, nor narrowly defined by, any particular field.

Autism is so much more than you can possibly imagine, beyond any interpretation or definition. It is certainly not what you think it to be.

40

Nothing Special

Before enlightenment chop wood carry water,
after enlightenment, chop wood carry water.

Zen proverb

Whenever you believe yourself to be special, you create distance between yourself and others.

The deeper reality is that there is no separation between you and 'others'. Paradoxically, when you can affirm the uniqueness of your journey, and accept yourself exactly as you are, you will then loosen your attachment to the small and contracted person you believe yourself to be. In affirming this deeper reality the smokescreen that is the finite perception you hold of yourself gradually lifts like the mist at the dawn of a new day.

Your small self, that some may call your ego, delights in feeling special and different, and forever seeks to feel secure and safe in a world that is overwhelming. However, you experience the spiritual life as a series of lessons in which you respect and value your human needs, whilst at the same time affirming your true identity as a Soul. This is your practice; this is your life.

Whilst it is true that being on the autism spectrum can at times make you feel different, this feeling that you are special is ultimately divisive – it sets you apart and prevents you from moving beyond this limited identification of who you really are. Understanding the part autism plays in your life has been very important, for you could not move on until you could consciously accept it. In so doing, you were able to start letting go of conforming to a world that was forever beyond your grasp, and releasing into something infinitely wider: containers are essential until you are ready to blossom.

This process was so liberating – conforming had been so constricting, yet you could not move beyond what you were unable to either name or bless with presence. The same could be true with respect to working through trauma.

The drama that surrounded you in the past has abated. Today you live creatively with your limitations, but you also live more abundantly through your gifts. One of the greatest of these is knowing that nothing in your life has been wasted; as Thich Nhat Hanh says, 'No Mud, No Lotus.'

For you the contemplative life is like cultivating an interior garden, and you have spent many years lovingly tending to this garden within. Now your work is simply continuing to tend and 'simply be' in the garden, being nothing special.

41

There Is Nothing New

History merely repeats itself.
It has all been done before.
Nothing under the sun is truly new.

Ecclesiastes

When you were a teenager your father would delight in saying to you, 'Son, never forget, whatever you have written on the toilet wall, I've written before you.' Although you were too young at the time to grasp where he was going with this, today this story delights you for its wonderful humour and also for the profound truth that the story inadvertently conveys.

As a writer you know that whatever you write has been written before. No longer do you strive to write the next best thing that never really is; you know it has all been said before. Having this perspective frees you up, like diving into an ocean and drifting upon its tide, not caring where it all leads, but revelling in the ecstasy and the adventure of it all.

You know that ultimately you are not the doer of your actions. 'Whether seeing, hearing, touching, smelling, eating, walking, sleeping, or breathing, the knower of truth should think, "I do nothing at all,"' as it says in the *Bhagavad Gita*. The challenge you face is to play the game of duality, which naturally includes making choices, whilst at the same time affirming the ultimate dimension, 'I do nothing at all.'

Your small and contracted self is convinced it has free will, and in a relative sense, it has. It is from out of this relative egoic universe that your small self believes it rules supreme. However, if you live your life with an open heart, the universe will always find ways to confront you with your vulnerability in order for you to learn the lessons you are here to learn.

It is here that you are given one of the greatest invitations, an opportunity to glimpse the ultimate dimension, the infinite Self within. This dropping from your head into your heart is never *your* doing, you are taken there by grace, and by grace alone you will be transformed.

The paradox here is that whilst all this drama is being played out within you, your deeper Self can never be overshadowed, for it is free from the bondage of time and the duality inherent within the play of your human incarnation. This was brought home to you one day when your son, then aged six or seven, said, 'Dad, if I wasn't who I am now, who or where would I be?' This beautifully innocent question left you feeling that your son intuitively and naturally identified with something infinitely greater, beyond the form he was in at that moment.

When you can break free from your conditioned mind and drop into your heart, you are able to break free of suffering and duality. Here you are able to see with new eyes, yet this very new way of seeing is in fact older than you can possibly imagine.

…and then, the Blackbird Sings

'Hope' is the thing with feathers
That perches in the soul
And sings the tune without the words
And never stops at all…

Emily Dickinson

Birds have taught you how to wait. You simply cannot just rush out into the marshes and expect to see a bittern straight away. Nor can you expect to hear the evocative call of a curlew the moment you arrive on the bank overlooking the estuary. The contemplative life is no different. You have to be patient and wait and simply be open to what is. Then the real drama can reveal itself.

Nature offers you a sanctuary from the endless noise and sensory over-stimulation of modern life in the city. It is for this reason that you spend much of your free time walking in wild and secluded places and simply being with birds. Your heart even skips a beat when you hear the goldfinches' liquid tinkling 'whit-a-whit-a-whit' as they pass overhead amidst the city's urban noise. The sound of birdsong in the city can transform your day. Birds become like little angels that remind you repeatedly to create a space for grace.

In Aldous Huxley's novel *Island*, specially trained mynah birds would loudly screech out, 'Here and now... Here and now!' at random intervals to remind the inhabitants on this imaginary utopian island to bring their attention to the present moment.

Birdsong is for you the sweetest of all alarm calls, waking you up out of the city's sleepwalking trance and into who you really are. It is as though they are saying to you, 'I'm here now. Are you?' Being on the autism spectrum your senses are so vibrantly alive and attuned to the smallest of details that you can find so utterly compelling. Yet what makes them so is their relationship to the oneness that permeates everything, the finite dancing within the infinite. Your experience finds great resonance in the words of Juan Mascaró in his introduction to the *Bhagavad Gita*, when he says, 'everything in creation can be a mathematical equation for the mind and a song of love for the soul'. This statement holds both aspects of your nature – your intellect and your soul.

So compelling is life at times that you can feel exhausted and overwhelmed by the whole drama of it all. There is just too much stimulation from all your thoughts, feelings, sensations, and life's events, which all collude together in their attempt to seduce you into analysing everything at once. It is as though you are trying to work out all the mysteries in life en route to the Underground station. And then, the blackbird sings...reminding you of the deeper reality that there is nothing you really need to work out at all, and there is nowhere you really need to go. Acknowledging this, you still go on your way, but certainly walk a lot slower and with greater lightness in your step.

43

Being an Elder

Our life is love, and peace, and tenderness; and bearing one with another, and forgiving one another, and not laying accusations one against another; but praying one for another, and helping one another up with a tender hand.

Isaac Penington

After attending the Quaker meeting for worship at Westminster regularly, it came as a great shock to be nominated as an elder. Yet after much discernment, you decided to take on the role.

Being an elder and having responsibility for the spiritual life of the community was not a role you ever imagined you would find yourself taking on. Your immediate thought was, 'I can't do this. I can't spell and I am unable to process and communicate written and verbal information sufficiently well for me to accept such a position of responsibility.' Another fear that was floating around in your mind was, 'Am I really qualified to take this responsibility on?' Slowly, both these fears softened the more you were able to express what your limitations were to fellow elders.

Gradually the disqualifying thoughts subsided. However, no sooner were you beginning to adjust to the role of elder, than another problem became apparent, that of your social anxiety. Being on the autism spectrum, social interaction has always been difficult for you. Before you took on the responsibility of being an elder, meeting for worship offered you the perfect hiding place from the drama of the world. You simply slipped into meeting and then slipped out again, and whilst you often valued the small conversations with fellow Friends over coffee, your interaction with them was still limited to what was comfortable for you.

But now the game had changed, for you were expected to sit on the front row, and in so doing you felt as though you were 'on show'. Often you would feel self-conscious and awkward, like a water rail might feel when forced out of its natural habitat in the reeds by adverse weather conditions. Eventually, you were able to respond to your awkwardness quietly through mindful awareness, and as a result the level of discomfort lessened. You became aware that the joy you were receiving through giving service as an elder greatly outweighed the awkwardness.

This beautiful reflection on being an elder by the Massachusetts Quaker, Danelle LaFlower, captures your heart and reminds you just what a gift it is to be an elder:

> *Feeling god's pain – not necessarily in a negative sense.*
> *Willing to accept a constant state of grace.*
> *The visible presence of god.*
> *Willing to be lost, depressed, afraid and still act and still be*
> *   faithful.*
> *Continual remembering. A channel, reflector, deflector,*
> *   funnel.*
> *My own humanness*
> *Weakness, etc. . . .*

You regard it as a great privilege to serve as an elder at Westminster meeting, to be accepted in spite of your many limitations, and to play your part in upholding the spiritual life of the community.

44

Allowing Messiness

Doing nothing is better than being busy doing nothing.

Lao Tzu

Both messiness and routines have a part to play in keeping your life in good balance.

Your senses are hyper-attuned to the world around you. At times you feel as though everything is illuminated with an intensity that can be as overwhelming as it can be beautiful.

As a person on the autism spectrum, your brain has a very limited capacity to filter and process incoming information. It all just comes blazing right at you, as though you are living permanently in the fast lane of a sensory motorway. Consequently, you have developed routines and systems to help you to have a certain degree of control over life.

In the spiritual life, as with psychotherapy and recovery, control is generally seen as something negative, or something that stands in the way of growth. Whilst this may hold a certain degree of truth for you, this by no means tells the whole truth, because without your highly adaptive skills, your life would be totally unmanageable. However, you know well that what you ultimately attempt to control ends up controlling you, and that perfectionism only takes you to an illusionary world which can stand in the way of presence and being with what *is*.

Your longing to be more in the world, but not so overwhelmed by it, has drawn you deeper into the contemplative life and greatly influenced and shaped the life you have today. It requires great skill and practice to put a spacious awareness around the dramas that confront you in life. A useful illustration of the sheer hard work and effort required to achieve this is that of manually operating a car jack, in order to create a space underneath the car to tend to a blown-out tyre. Contemplative practice is like this in that it assists you in creating space in order to attend to what is going on within you when things break down.

Drawing from this well of mindfulness in everyday life will inevitably confront you with the perfectionist side of your nature. However, 'being' in the messiness of life is simply a spiritual practice in itself, in the same way that your routines and systems of organising are a natural part of your way of being functional in the world. In understanding this, you are able to start lovingly holding these two parts, both the messy and the ordered, which, until recently, have been in conflict with each other.

Allowing messiness is in essence allowing life to be life. Meeting life with presence transforms the messiness of drama into dharma, the Hindu principle of cosmic order.

It is for this reason that you dedicate yourself to meditation and the contemplative life.

45

Healing the Wounds
of Separation

The wound is the place where the Light enters you.

Rumi

The child psychologist D.W. Winnicott famously said, 'It is a joy to be hidden, and a disaster not to be found.' At first thought, you would assume that this deeply thought-provoking statement is relevant only to the children's game of hide-and-seek and the psychological elements he derived from it. However, probe beneath the surface and you can see that this 'hide-and-seek' game is a potent metaphor for waking up to your true nature, and that this true nature resides within the deepest part of your 'being human'.

Like the parables of Jesus, the *Bhagavad Gita* and *Upanishads* can wake you up like a Zen kōan offering you a poetic and profound insight into this 'hide-and-seek' or 'cosmic dance', moving you on from a dualistic mindset and into unitive awareness itself. You have suffered, not so much because of the many painful dramas that have come your way, but because of your inability to wake up and see the deeper drama within the drama of being human itself.

There are many layers of reality, just like denial, that you will need to uncover. Just as snakes shed their skins, you, too, will have to let go of the attachment to the person you thought yourself to be. Each 'shedding' or 'uncovering' is like a purifying fire or rite of passage, whereby you simply let go of what you no longer need. Holding on to what you do not need just gets in the way of waking up.

However, you cannot do this 'waking up' alone, for the person you think yourself to be will not give up that easily. Let's face it, who but a saint can laugh as they go voluntarily into the fire of purification? For this is what it means to really heal the wounds of separation. The whole point of life, just like the game of hide-and-seek, is to be truly found.

46

A Doorway into Truth

Plunge into the Truth, find out who the Teacher is.

Kabir

There have been many influences that have illuminated your spiritual path, including the great religious founders such as Jesus, Buddha, Krishna and Lao Tzu, numerous saints and holy people, and meditative practices from a variety of traditions.

Of these, it has been Eastern philosophy, and particularly Advaita Vedanta, that has in more recent times been significant in widening your perceptions. This has enabled you to see not only the profound truths in Jesus's teachings at greater depth, but also the essential truths within the wisdom teachings of the major religious traditions. Out of this soulful quest you came upon the teachings of Ramana Maharshi, the sage of Arunachala, who is widely regarded as one of the greatest spiritual teachers of the modern era. His teaching on Self-enquiry, and the way in which he would transmit his teachings through silence, had a remarkable effect on people whilst he was alive, just as they do on you today.

Whichever way you travel up the mountain, sooner or later you reach a point where you have to accept that your thinking mind can only take you so far. Here you are confronted with mystery. How you sit with this mystery will determine so much with respect to your maturity in the spiritual life. It is into this experience that

you have been drawn deeper and deeper into the eyes of
Ramana Maharshi.

Whilst many wise teachers have touched your heart,
Ramana Maharshi has penetrated it. His practice of
Self-enquiry, using the mind to move beyond the mind,
alongside the practice of devotion and surrender, has
become a way that holds both aspects of your nature, the
head and the heart.

'Pursue the inquiry, "Who am I" relentlessly,' says
Ramana: 'Analyse your entire personality. Try to find out
where the I-thought begins. Go on with your meditations.
Keep turning your attention within. One day the wheel of
thought will slow down and an intuition will mysteriously
arise. Follow that intuition, let your thinking stop, and
it will lead eventually to the goal.' This practice of
Self-enquiry is perhaps the most powerful means whereby
you can experience the deeper reality at play within the
play of life.

Through Ramana Maharshi's eyes, you see a doorway
into a timeless and eternal reality which is your true and
eternal nature, which can never really be spoken about,
only ever experienced.

47

Spiritual Bypassing

The ego will not go in gladness and with caresses.
It must be chased with sorrow drowned in tears.

Old Persian saying

So easy it is to use spirituality as a defence against being simply human. This can often result in creating a false identity of being 'spiritual' at the expense of genuine growth and progress in the spiritual life – this you know from your personal experience.

You are no stranger to having to defend yourself against overwhelming psychological pain. Over the years, you have come to understand well the very human need in times of crisis to contract around your hurt and 'de-press' it all down. Out of sight, out of mind; not in your conscious awareness, but ever present in your body. What resists persists, and such unmet suffering will always come at a cost until you can bring it to the light of loving awareness. This is soul work.

This is why spirituality for you is all about letting go. Yet you cannot let go of something you are unaware you are holding on to. This was especially true for you with respect to being on the autism spectrum. It is for this reason that you have fully embraced psychotherapy and recovery work alongside contemplative practice. You know from your own experience, as well as through accompanying others in your role as a spiritual guide, that you simply cannot transcend the unhealed elements within you until you can meet your own suffering with presence.

Spiritual bypassing, like magical thinking, can be one of the most subtle and complex ways in which you can fool yourself, and others, into believing you are how you would wish yourself to be. The much-loved spiritual teacher Ram Dass tells the story of how he was trying too hard to be spiritual, 'phoney holy', as he would call it, and playing the game of being further along the path than where he really was. Then his friend said to him, 'You're in school. Why don't you try taking the curriculum?' In other words, you have a human form, therefore allow yourself to be human.

The person you believe yourself to be would be a most unhelpful companion on this journey into who you really are. Your small self fears its demise and eventual death, therefore it will use everything it has at its disposal to resist the truth coming through. Consequently, the ego always has some game or other going on.

Being able to be intimate with yourself, and accepting yourself just the way you are, including your fear and grief, has proven a very effective way of not falling into the trap of spiritual bypassing. By observing what is going on with tenderness, and without judgement, you can slowly awaken into truth.

48

Dancing with the Elephant in the Room

But recovery of soul begins when we can take to heart our own family fate and find in it the raw material for our own soul work.

Thomas Moore

Your parents, like many of their generation, grew up in the shadow of two devastating world wars, the consequences of which left deep emotional scars. There were to be personal losses too, which all contributed to a shadow being cast over your entire family. Unspoken sadness became the elephant in the room, which had a tangible presence in every area of home life.

As a child growing up, you watched your family being consumed by relentless activity. It was as if the unbearable agony of sadness weighed so heavily within their closely guarded hearts that any slowing down would allow the ghosts of the past to catch up and devour them. The more your family attempted to outrun this invisible 'enemy', the more it simply took up residence in their hearts.

For many years you used to have a recurring dream, which you came to interpret as conveying the enormity of despair and denial that you all lived under. A passenger plane is plucked out of the sky and comes crashing down into your back garden. Dismembered bodies, trapped within the tangled wreckage of the plane, become strewn all over the perfectly manicured lawn. You become agitated, scream, you are waving your hands frantically and pointing to the children whose bodies are being crushed in the wreckage, beside themselves with distress. Yet your parents cannot hear you, and they appear not to acknowledge the entire drama within their own garden. Your father simply continues to mow the lawn, your mother is watering the rose garden and your sister is studying inside behind closed doors.

As with many families where there is collective repression, a scapegoat is often created on which to project the family's own shortcomings. There were many reasons why you became this scapegoat in your family, the obvious one being your autism, with its very different way of behaving and of perceiving reality. There was also a deeper issue in play – that you always knew in your heart that you were living a lie, playing a game the rules of which were alien to who you really were. Conformity to the rules of this game was of paramount importance so as to avoid being hurt. However, complete conformity meant a certain death. But you did not come into this life just to survive it. You came into this life to live it.

As you continued playing the game of survival, you unconsciously created a persona of being good. Whilst this 'being good' mask lessened the humiliation you received, it also cast you back into the collective shadow of all the original 'wreckage' and trauma of unspoken loss. However, it seemed that for each dark cave in which you buried your past, there was the other part of you, your deeper Self, which carried a ball of string, as in the ancient Greek legend of Theseus, marking your path so as to lead you home when the conditions were right.

Your burning desire for truth, combined with life's events, was eventually to lead you back into those dark shadowy caves. It was here, in the depths of such darkness, that you found the courage and skilful support whereby you were to bear the tension created by the original split in your psyche, your 'crucifixion'. In so doing you were confronted with the overwhelming power of your family's shadow.

It took many years of dancing with this elephant in the room before it could reveal to you its secrets. When it did there followed a grief so all-consuming that it changed your entire relationship with yourself and with your family, to the extent that there was nothing left to forgive and only love remained.

49

Autism as an Awakening

What you want to overcome you must first of all submit to...

Lao Tzu

In your autobiography, *A Painful Gift*, you brought out into the open the enormous struggle of living your life within the cloud of unknowing that you were on the autism spectrum. As the years passed you came to see that there really was nothing special about your own story. Many people just like yourself had reached middle age depressed, exhausted and overwhelmed by unknowingly over-compensating and adapting to being on the autism spectrum.

It is quite ironic that what you regard as one of your greatest achievements, your adaptive skills, became your greatest impediment and barrier to being diagnosed and getting the help you so desperately needed. You simply became too convincing behind your persona of normality for the depth of struggle and heartbreak to reveal itself. It seemed that for every humiliation you received as a child, your mask of so-called normality became ever more fused to your being. However, what once served to protect you from abuse and humiliation was now constricting and crushing.

Being a spiritual guide has helped you to see that people all have defences and personas, and that they wear them like garments of clothing. However, you have learned from your own experience that you can suffer a great deal when you become over-attached to the masks you wear, to the extent that you lose touch with who it is that is looking through the mask.

When the mask falls, so, too, can the sadness that gave birth to this protective layer. In tenderly holding this grief, a doorway can be found that will set you free.

Your experience of being diagnosed with high-functioning autism was life-changing. It was like a moment of enlightenment whereby you felt as though you were given your humanity back. At first there was euphoria — the overwhelming joy of your struggle being seen and given its rightful name. 'The beginning of wisdom is to call things by their proper name,' said Confucius.

However, a deeper truth was soon to reveal itself that could not be so easily diagnosed or given a name to. This deeper truth was that you simply lost the person you believed yourself to be. This falling away of the concept you held of yourself after your diagnosis happened imperceptibly at first, until one day it just fell from you like a redundant skin. Into this drama came the question, 'If I am not this self that has been constructed out of survival, then who am I?' At the time you were bewildered and mystified as to what was happening to you. Being intimate with and integrating this experience took some time and skill. As a result a very new way of relating to yourself and the world began to unfold.

Today you can look back at your diagnosis with autism as a moment that changed your life in more ways than you could have possibly imagined at the time.

50

The Second Arrow

Pain is inevitable, but suffering is optional.

Buddhist saying

The Buddha's parable of the second arrow has much to teach you about being more present within yourself, in a world that at times can be extremely overwhelming.

The first arrow the Buddha talks of symbolises the pain that is inseparably a part of life. However, the second arrow he refers to is the very unskilful way in which we react and contract around that pain. 'If you get struck by an arrow, do you then shoot another arrow into yourself?'

This 'second arrow' could be anything that somehow stands in the way of your recovery or healing. The essence of the story is that it is the holding on to pain and not the pain itself that causes suffering.

Your tendency is to get lost in a cycle of reactivity. However, in order to be able to step out of that cycle you first need to become aware that you are in it. This is not easy, especially if your heart is pulsating and adrenaline is flowing through you and influencing every cell in your body. However, with practice you are learning to lean into the discomfort that can often confront you in contemplative practice, and to attend to and befriend that part of you that so cries out to be seen, understood and held.

It has been your experience that it is impossible to be deeply present in life until you can be present with this wounded part of you that has recoiled into itself out of immense fear. The extent to which you can hold tenderly your pain determines the extent to which you can move beyond your attachment to it. In affirming the pain with tenderness, thus softening your attachment to it, you create a spacious awareness around the drama of clinging and the suffering that comes from such holding on.

You cannot insulate yourself from the pain that is a part of life, but through being mindful you learn to hold everything in a more spacious and loving awareness. To remain blind to the second arrow is to remain blind to your true nature.

51

Coming Home to 'Being'

Where thou art, that is home.

Emily Dickinson

Coming home is one thing, and 'being' at home can be quite another.

Your very earliest experience of home was harrowing and disturbing, right from experiencing heroin abuse whilst in the womb. This was followed by the neglectful approach to baby care in the Crusade of Rescue mother and baby home, then the dysfunctional and alcoholic home that your adoptive parents offered you, and then the psychiatric home you were admitted to in adolescence. Home for you was 'no place like home'.

Your childhood was spent living in what felt like a series of war zones in which you lived on the front line in a war that never seemed to end. You dug yourself in deep, kept your head low, and expected death to come upon you at any time. The effect this had on you was devastating.

This chronic lack of safety and understanding drew you deeper into yourself, as you sought a refuge where you could find a place of security and calm. As a result, 'being' at home has always been a struggle for you, because of your need to over-control your home environment rather than allowing yourself to simply 'be' within its walls. Even today, after a quarter of a century of befriending this wounded part of yourself, you still feel so much happier in other people's homes than you do in your own.

'Coming home' for you was never going to be easy, as the ghosts of your childhood had left a deep impression upon you, determining so much of your behaviour and the decisions you have made in your life. Everywhere you went, you carried deep within yourself this internal state of dereliction and abandonment.

The image of a soldier coming home from war has always resonated with you, for the simple reason that it is only when the drama surrounding trauma abates that the feelings underlying it can come to the surface. Understanding this, and holding with great tenderness this wounded part of you, has brought enormous healing, and you have been fortunate to have had many wise guides accompanying you in this coming home, this movement into 'being'.

Finding your home in the present moment is the surest foundation on which to build your spiritual life. Jesus's parable of the wise and foolish builders comes immediately to mind here. So easy it is to take false refuge in the drama of the world at the expense of being in the timeless and eternal present.

52

Thought for the Day

You are what your deep,
driving desire is.
As your desire is, so is your will.
As your will is, so is your deed.
As your deed is, so is your destiny.

Brihadaranyaka Upanishad

Each morning, just before you fully awake from sleep, even before your eyelids have opened, you find yourself between two very contrasting states of consciousness. It is here, suspended between sleep and waking, that you gently inhale, whispering the sound 'I', then exhale the sound 'am'. 'I am' – imitating the sound of the breath, the first and last words as we enter and leave the world.

It is the timing of this early morning 'I am' that is so crucial. For to wait until the wheels of cognition kick in and your thoughts, feelings and sensations come more fully into play will only weaken the potency of this proclamation of who you really are. Starting your day in such a way has proved to be worth more than a thousand hours of formal prayer. The reason for this is that even by the time you have made it to the bathroom, and long before you have even put the kettle on, your thoughts will have already become clouded by habitual thinking, and the pressing need to plan and organise your day and to be in control. Ironically it is this very same need to be in control that you will earnestly be praying to hand over when you have eventually found the time to do so through formal prayer.

In the final years of your father's life, you would hold his hand and watch him moving between dreaming, deep sleep and waking states. Many times you would watch his face soften, followed by the releasing of tension in his hand as he drifted off into sleep. Then slowly he would be aroused, himself suspended between deep sleep and waking consciousness. You would watch his eyes open ever so slowly, followed by a radiant smile which, like the sun, would fill the entire room. He had awakened, though he had not yet turned his attention to the virtual horror show of thoughts running through his mind. It seemed as though his senses were not attuned to anything other than the present moment. These treasured moments lasted only seconds, and then his face would contort with despair and his hand would contract like a vice around your own, as he became almost immediately embroiled in the despair into which his thoughts were leading him.

When you look deeply into the nature of your own suffering, you can see that your own predicament of how to live creatively with your own thoughts is really no different from your father's, or anyone else's for that matter.

Your early morning 'I am' creates a space in which you can take a peep underneath the veil of thoughts, and briefly touch the deeper reality that lies beyond the virtual reality of your thoughts and beliefs, and even the concept you hold of yourself.

53

You Are the Music

And those who were seen dancing were thought to be insane by those who could not hear the music.

Friedrich Nietzsche

As a musician, as with being a writer, you spend your life diving into the depths of your being in search of raw materials through which to communicate your ideas to the world.

Whilst words are for you a labour of love requiring hard work and effort, your experience of creating music can only really be achieved through the act of playing. You cannot 'work' music; you simply play it. There is for you no image that conveys this so beautifully than the image of Krishna, the cosmic musician playing his transcendental flute, drawing people deeper within themselves, revealing to them their true and timeless nature.

In the stillness of a Quaker meeting for worship, you can hear the music in the gathered silence shared amongst Friends. In the same way that the written word can punctuate a sheet of paper, spoken ministry can punctuate the silence, the very silence from which everything comes and to which it will eventually return. In this context you can see every soul as a musical note being played out within the unceasing eloquence of silence itself. Silence and music dancing as one.

As a child you attended mass regularly with your family, and you can recall vividly today how captivated you were by the priest singing the Eucharistic Prayer.

Such sacred and devotional singing meant so much more to you then than even the Eucharist. For you the spirit and presence of Christ flowed effortlessly and freely within the music itself, which seemed to linger in the air with the frankincense. As a child, it seemed to you that the music could not be contained, unlike the Eucharist that had the strictest of rules attached to it and sat so lonely in its golden ornate cage.

Today you see that nothing can be separated, that everything is infused with God's presence just as it is, and because of this, everything *is* music. However, on a very human level, whilst everything may be music, that's not to say that it is always sweet or harmonious. As you write these very words, a man has sat down right opposite you, here, in the rose garden in Hyde Park. As he talked on his mobile phone, his affected mannerisms and elevated voice cut through the tranquillity you had enjoyed whilst composing this piece of writing. This is the challenge of living life in London, where cars, sirens, pneumatic drills and contrasting accents are endlessly being 'played out' to an overwhelming degree.

Through recognising and allowing what *is*, however discordant this may be, you can then see the music in everything that is going on around you. In so doing, you come to fully appreciate the wise words of Alan Watts when he said, 'Life is like music for its own sake. We are living in an eternal now, and when we listen to music, we are not listening to the past, we are not listening to the future, we are listening to an expanded present.'

54

Sweet Etty Hillesum

I may face cruelty and deprivation the likes of which I cannot imagine in even my wildest fantasies. Yet all this is as nothing to the immeasurable expanse of my faith in God and my inner receptiveness.

Etty Hillesum

In your living room you have a framed picture of a woman whose soul you feel is inseparably entwined with your own. The woman's name is Etty Hillesum, otherwise known as the 'Mystic of the Holocaust'.

Etty was a young Dutch Jewish woman, who documented her interior life with uncompromising honesty in her pursuit of meaning and truth. All her writings were composed in the shadow of the Holocaust, before and during the Nazi occupation of Amsterdam, and then after her arrival at Westerbork transit camp. Like yourself, Etty's spirit could not be contained by any theology, dogma, church or synagogue. She was her own person and a free spirit in the truest sense of the word.

Throughout your life you have been deeply drawn to the lives of the saints, mystics, sages and devout holy people of many traditions. However, what makes Etty's writings so accessible and so refreshing for you is that she did not bypass her human desires and longings. On the contrary, she held them all up to the light and in so doing they became the raw materials from which her interior life would blossom.

Etty saw such unspeakable horror in the camps in which she was imprisoned and yet, right at the centre of it all, she found love and meaning. Her writings became infused with such intense mystical fervour, whilst at the same time they conveyed the dignity and human warmth she never lost. She came to see what few could ever imagine.

'Living and dying, sorrow and joy, the blisters on my feet and the jasmine behind the house, the persecution, the unspeakable horrors – it is all as one in me, and I accept it all as one mighty whole and begin to grasp it better if only to myself, without being able to explain it to anyone else how it all hangs together.'

When your life is overwhelming, when the residue of your past weighs you down, you often take Etty's diaries off the bookshelf, read a chapter or two and then leave the book out on the table. This brings you such comfort. Sometimes you even take her picture down off your wall and gaze into her eyes, just like you do with the picture of Ramana Maharshi, the sage of Arunachala. Etty's eyes hold such power. When you cannot see beyond your finite way of perceiving, you look into the eyes of those who can. What is reflected back is who you really are. Through Etty's eyes you see the play of timelessness within time itself reflected back in you. Here there is no separation, there is no separate self; everything is One.

Etty died on the 30th of November 1943 in the gas chambers of Auschwitz. The final entry in her diary reads, 'We should be willing to act as a balm for all wounds.'

55

It's All Perfect

...we have become marked by suffering for a whole lifetime.
And yet life, in its unfathomable depths, is so wonderfully
good...

Etty Hillesum

How is it really possible to remain present when in
overwhelming pain, when suffering has ravaged your
strength and the fragile threads of your faith are in tatters?
Can you really put your hand on your heart and say, 'It's
all perfect'?

Staying with the lessons that suffering can teach you
is no easy undertaking. To keep your heart open and allow
your vulnerability to show itself, whilst being alive to the
mystery of it all, seems more like the path for a saint rather
than for a simple human being like yourself.

However, you have come to know that even in the
most harrowing of circumstances, there is a part of you
which suffering cannot reach. This part of you is very real,
yet often silent. It is from out of this deep silence, a place
beyond the ability of the rational mind to comprehend,
that you live your life.

Often it feels as though there are two realities being
played out, the ego and the soul. You see the relationship
between your ego and your soul as like a dance, the
dance of form and formlessness within the one reality
that permeates everything. Seeing life in this way comes
naturally to you and in affirming this deeper reality, it

helps you to soften the intensity of drama around your thinking mind's preoccupation with disease and death.

To enter into this dance with presence takes the most extraordinary discipline and a great deal of patience and persistence. Here you are reminded of the famous saying from Zen teacher Robert Aitken when he said, 'Enlightenment is an accident; and practice makes us accident prone.' Becoming more accident-prone means many things to you, not least of which is starting by slowing down as a means of coming awake to a deeper reality. Creating a space for grace. This enables you to weave the fruits of formal meditation practice into the dramas that come your way, even recent events as dramatic as your father's agonisingly long and drawn-out illness, the suicide of one close friend, and the terminal illness of another very dear friend.

It is easy to see that everything is grace, that everything is perfect, when the going is good, but to see grace in the midst of suffering, either your own, or of those you love, can be overwhelmingly difficult and takes an enormous leap of faith.

Perfection is not something to work towards, for everything is perfect just as it is. All you need to do is to learn how to get out of the way and surrender to what *is*.

56

Using Your Stories Up

The extent to which you can lovingly hold your stories will become the extent to which you will ultimately be free from them.

Christopher Goodchild

You are a Soul through which your stories, the narrative of your life, endlessly flow.

Your practice is to watch this continuously flowing drama of your past experiences with the utmost compassion and dispassion, neither over-identifying with, nor denying, the stories that have shaped the person you are today. To dismiss your stories, your past experiences, before you have held them tenderly in your heart and listened deeply to their secrets, is to miss the whole point as to why you are undertaking this human journey.

With each retelling, your story loosens its unconscious grip upon you, and takes you to those frozen places within, enabling a thawing out of painful and traumatic memories. This experience has often been deeply distressing for you, taking you out of your mind literally, and into the physicality of the experience itself. This 'being' in the rawness of your suffering, yet not getting tangled up in the story from which it originated, has become a rite of passage, a movement from your head into your heart.

To 'be' in this place of vulnerability has often felt as though you are going to die, and in a sense, that is exactly what happens. It is from out of this psychological death that the concept of the person you believed yourself to be collapses, then the stories of your past can fall back into the silence from which they came.

Your early religious instruction and education conditioned you to believe that all the 'good stuff', which included spirituality, was somewhere to be found 'out there', and if only you worked hard enough, and long enough, you would find this elusive happiness. However, this preoccupation with 'out there' came at the cost of your interior life, and of valuing yourself deeply as a human being.

You came to see that there really was no 'out there' at all, and that the 'doing' that needed to be done was very subtle. This entailed not so much a discipline of learning more, but instead a willingness to unlearn everything that you had ever been taught. This included your understanding of the very nature of thought itself. In so doing you came to see that your thoughts are simply responding to nothing more than your past experiences. Learning to hold your stories more intimately and tenderly enables you to move beyond them.

Freed from your narrative and his-Story there is nothing to overcome. Nothing to strive for. Nothing to believe in. Just simply being what *is*.

57

It's All an Open Secret

It is everywhere, though we see it not.
Just so, dear one, the Self is everywhere, within all things...

Upanishads

You cannot find what is already there – Divinity – though what you can do is wake up and realise this. However, you cannot do this waking up alone, for it is a process, a journey, and it takes as long as it takes until it carries you to the pathless path of simply what *is*.

The road is perilous that leads to truth, and this you know very well through your experiences in life. It is for this reason that you have taken heed of the age-old wisdom in finding a teacher, submitting yourself completely to their guidance and remaining faithful to their teaching. You have found many wise teachers who can point the way, though as yet, very few who embody the way.

Truth is in essence a pathless path, and yet, like most people, you have needed to journey outside of yourself in order to come home to your Self. The play of duality has been as colourful and as compelling for you as it would be for anyone else.

An important key to the spiritual life is acquiring the skill to see things as they are, and not simply as they appear to you, just like the rainbow in the sky appears to be real, yet it is merely a play of light. For you this process of looking beyond appearances and into a deeper reality started with you doing quite the opposite. So convinced were you that the image you were projecting outwards was the only thing that mattered, that you were denying your entitlement to being human, by not allowing yourself the right to express your feelings or human needs. In so doing you unknowingly created a persona of being spiritual, a 'spiritual good guy', attempting to play God before you had any real understanding of what it meant to be fully human. With hindsight you can see that you were taking spiritual flight, bypassing what you needed to learn in order to authentically progress on your spiritual journey.

Whilst metaphors such as paths or journey can prove useful in the spiritual life, with their road signs at crossroads, roundabouts or diversions that help you take the right route, as you progress along the way they will simply disappear. Eventually you will arrive knowing there is no 'where' to go, and no 'thing' you really need to do. This is impossible to convey through words, as these opening lines in the *Tao Te Ching* show:

> *The Tao that can be spoken is not the true Tao*
> *The name that can be named is not the eternal Name.*

Your identity is as a Soul, not merely as the roles you are playing out in the world, however much these roles can loosely define you. When you understand this, your roles can then pave the way, as opposed to obstructing the way.

All this helps you to see the open secret that is everywhere – that you are fully human and fully divine.

58

Eternally Grateful

I would maintain that thanks are the highest form of thought;
and that gratitude is happiness doubled by wonder.

G.K. Chesterton

Curiosity started you out on this journey, faith sustains it, and gratitude leads you all the way home.

As a person on the autism spectrum you have always found it extremely challenging relating to your peers and forming friendships. In addition to this, your difficulty in processing information, be it written or verbal, frequently results in you being dependent upon others to assist you in many areas of your life. This has often resulted in you being taken advantage of in some way or other. These experiences have all played their part in you finding it hard to trust people.

However, you have a very special friend today, whose presence you cannot imagine being without. This friend has taught you what trust is. This trust was not found overnight, but grew slowly from out of the many small and simple things you shared together over the years. Your friend simply gave you all the space you needed to just simply be who you are, and continues to do so. For she loves you just the way you are, and in so doing she has loved you into being yourSelf.

You have endless fun enjoying tomfoolery with your special friend. In the past, you never felt comfortable sharing with another person your idiosyncratic and absurd sense of humour. However, she seems to find it rather amusing, and you delight in making her laugh. Often you go to great lengths with your pranks, and sometimes the sole purpose of phoning her is simply to make her chuckle.

This book would not have been possible without your friend's help. She taught you how to write many years ago, and she has been devoted to helping you edit all your books ever since. However, her ability to draw you deeper into yourself, with her insightful and probing questions, has given this book an extra dimension that it would not have had otherwise.

Writing from such a deep place is one thing, yet 'being' with what you have written has always been the greater challenge, and one you have succeeded in fulfilling. In so doing you have come to see that you have not so much spent the last year writing a book; you have simply been hanging out on the spiritual plane, appearing to write a book with your soul friend. Naturally she would laugh at such a statement.

Your friendship, like the laughter and the words throughout this book, however carefully crafted, are simply pointers that lead beyond appearances and into something infinitely more expansive, and for all this you are eternally grateful.

Thank you, Katherine.

59

The Life that Never Ends

The truest end of life, is to know the life that never ends.

William Penn

By the time you have completed writing this meditation your father will have passed away.

These last seven years he has lain paralysed in bed, in a near-continuous state of despair, anxiety and overwhelming panic. As you watched him being hoisted up and down in order to be bathed and treated, you have often wondered how one can mentally endure such torment. His immobility and powerlessness have taken you back to your own earliest experiences of overwhelming trauma, where you too were powerless, immobile and totally dependent on others for your survival.

One valuable way of looking at suffering and death has been for you to enquire deeply within yourself, 'Who is it that is actually suffering?' and 'Who is it that actually dies?' Such a heartfelt enquiry, spontaneously asked, can have the power to loosen your attachment to your identification with your self merely as a physical human being.

If you cannot connect with that part of you that is timeless, eternal and beyond death, you will fear death, and this fear will plague you all your life. Consequently, over the years, you have approached many wise guides from many different paths and traditions, and listened deeply to their teachings, none more so than Ramana Maharshi. Through the light of his presence that emanates from him in your photographs, and through the practice of

Self-enquiry that he advocated, you have found a priceless treasure beyond words, called in the Hindu tradition the Self. The Western equivalent is the Soul. It is of little importance to you what it is called, but of enormous value to you in identifying with this integral part of your being.

Ramana summarised his thoughts on the subject of death by saying, 'If a man considers he is born, he cannot avoid the fear of death. Let him find out if he has been born or if the Self has any birth. He will discover that the Self always exists... Then you will abide in the ever-present inmost Self and be free from the idea of birth or the fear of death.'

Today your father passed away, yet before he breathed his last, you put your hand on his chest, and said, 'It is here, in the heart, that you shall forever live in me and I shall forever live in you. You are not this body that is falling from you, you are the Light that no suffering can ever put out.'

On a very human level, these last seven years watching your father suffer have been harrowing. Yet you have not turned away. Instead you have looked into the unbearable agony of it all and found love right at the centre. It is here, in the silence of the heart, that you have come to know the life that never ends.

60

The End of Words

The end of my labours has come. All that I have written appears to be as so much straw after the things that have been revealed to me.

St Thomas Aquinas

It took nearly a year of my life to write this book, and yet life itself could not be put on hold.

In this past year, I lost a dear friend to suicide. My mother died before I had even completed the Introduction.

My father died whilst I was writing one of the last chapters of the book. So too did the Benedictine monk, Patrick, my beloved friend. And two of my dearest friends have been diagnosed with terminal cancer. It is here, in the oncologist's waiting room, whilst accompanying one of these friends on his routine appointment, that I write and reflect upon this last year. The year in which I turned 50. A year I shall never forget.

'Pain is inevitable, but suffering is optional,' goes the saying. However, the reality is we all suffer. Yet whilst so much of my life has been shaped by loss and grief, it is ultimately not suffering or loss that defines who 'I am'. What I have lost cannot compare to what I have found.

This was apparent to me back in the spring when, whilst working on one of the meditations, I had sent a text message to a friend. In it I described how much the writing process was revealing to me, and how much joy I felt as a consequence. It went like this:

> I am alive with the writing. My heart is ablaze. I have my 'Why' to live and I am living it through today as though nothing else matters except these next 243 days ahead of me. It's not as if nothing ELSE matters, it's just that ALL that matters is somehow influencing everything in the way that makes my heart sing like the blackcap outside right now.
>
> All my writing pales into insignificance when I think of what it has taught me – using words in order to move beyond words.

As I write this last meditation, I hear the autumn leaves fall gracefully upon my caravan roof, whilst the leaves that remain on the trees cast their shadows, dancing out their patterns throughout the interior of my little caravan. It is here, to this sacred place in Norfolk, that I have travelled every other weekend, not only this year but over the last 15 years, to be with my son. It has become for me a pilgrimage. A pilgrimage of the heart.

Every dancing leaf that falls from the trees shows me that life itself is a sacramental dance, the steps of which can only ever really be learned by allowing myself to be most human and most vulnerable.

Today I can see that everything is perfect. Such perfection is not something that can be worked towards; it is simply a falling ever deeper into a profound acceptance of what *is*.

References

These are listed in the order in which they appear in the book.

Vyasa, V. (2008) *The Bhagavad Gita 2.12* (translated by L.L. Patton). London/New York: Penguin Group.

Meyer, M. (ed.) (2009) *The Nag Hammadi Scriptures: The Revised and Updated Translation of Sacred Gnostic Texts.* San Francisco, CA: HarperOne. [Gospel of Thomas]

Foreword

Dass, R. (2013) 'The Ram Dass interview: Smiling as he teaches about "Polishing the Mirror".' Read the Spirit. Available at www.readthespirit.com/explore/the-ram-dass-interview-on-polishing-the-mirror-you-cant-help-but-smile-hes-still-teaching-us, accessed on 18 November 2016.

Anonymous (1965) *Upanishads, Chandogya 6.8.7.* St Ives: Penguin Group.

Introduction

Dass, R. (2013) *Polishing the Mirror: How to Live from Your Spiritual Heart.* Louisville, CO: Sounds True Inc. [Lao Tzu]

America, K.F. (1980) 'Truth is a pathless land.' J. Krishnamurti online. Available at www.jkrishnamurti.org/about-krishnamurti/dissolution-speech.php, accessed on 18 November 2016. [Jiddu Krishnamurti]

Teilhard de Chardin, P. (2008) *The Phenomenon of Man.* New York: Harper Perennial.

Goodchild, C. (2009) *A Painful Gift: The Journey of a Soul with Autism.* London: Darton, Longman & Todd Ltd.

Meditation 1: Unclouded by Longing

Dass, R. (2013) *Polishing the Mirror: How to Live from Your Spiritual Heart.* Louisville, CO: Sounds True Inc. [Lao Tzu]

Thich Nhat Hanh (2010) *Reconciliation.* Berkeley, CA: Parallax Press.

Meditation 2: What Is It You Truly Long for?

Outler, A.C. (translator and editor) (2012 [1955]) *The Confessions of St Augustine.* New York: Courier Corporation (Dover Publications, Inc.). [St Augustine, Bishop of Hippo]

Lindahl, K. (2003) *Practising the Sacred Art of Listening.* Woodstock, VT: Skylight Paths Publishing. [Douglas Steere]

Meditation 3: The Light Behind the Watcher

(2009) *Quaker Faith and Practice, Fourth Edition.* Chapter 2, Section 2.18. London: Quaker Peace & Service. Available at http://qfp.quaker. org.uk/chapter/2, accessed on 14 December 2016. [George Fox, 1658]

Nisargadatta, S. (2012 [1973]) *I Am That.* Durham, NC: The Acorn Press, Chapter 42, p.188.

Meditation 4: The Quaker Way

(2009) *Quaker Faith and Practice, Fourth Edition.* Chapter 26, Section 26.1 (Advices, 1964). London: Quaker Peace & Service.

Rimbaud, A. (1975 [1967]) *Arthur Rimbaud, Complete Works* (translated by P. Schmidt). New York: Harper & Row, 'The Drunken Boat'.

Meditation 5: The Sorrowful Price of Freedom

(2009) *Quaker Faith and Practice, Fourth Edition.* Chapter 19, Section 19.03. London: Quaker Peace & Service. Available at http://qfp. quaker.org.uk/passage/19-03, accessed on 14 December 2016. [George Fox, 1647]

Old Hebrew saying, Menachem Mendel of Kotzk. Available at www. goodreads.com/quotes/65442-there-is-nothing-so-whole-as-a-broken-heart, accessed on 24 February 2017.

Jones, R.A. (ed.) (2009) *The Essential Henri Nouwen.* Boston, MA: Shambala. [Henri Nouwen]

Meditation 6: Befriending Your 'Black Dog'

(2009) *Quaker Faith and Practice, Fourth Edition.* Chapter 21, Section 21.65. London: Quaker Peace & Service. Available at http://qfp. quaker.org.uk/passage/21-65, accessed on 14 December 2016. [James Nayler]

Meditation 7: Allowing Your Body to Speak Its Mind

Bly, R. (ed.) (1976) *Kabir: Ecstatic Poems.* Boston, MA: Beacon Press. [Kabir]

Meditation 8: Giving In but Not Giving Up

Shakespeare, W. (1990 [1982]) *The Complete Works of William Shakespeare: Hamlet, Act III, Scene 1*. London: Hennewood Publications Ltd.

Meditation 9: The World as a Stage

Shakespeare, W. (1990) *The Complete Works of William Shakespeare: As You Like It, Act II, Scene VII*. London: Chancellor Press.

Teilhard de Chardin, P. (2008) *The Phenomenon of Man*. New York: Harper Perennial.

Ambler, R. (2010) *The Light Within – Then and Now: A Talk to the Quaker Universalist Conference at Woodbrooke 13 March 2010*. Available at www.lancsquakers.org.uk/light-within.pdf, accessed on 18 November 2016. [George Fox]

Meditation 11: To Love What *Is*

Hunt, D.S. (2004) *Only This! Poems and Reflections by Dorothy S. Hunt*. San Francisco, CA: San Francisco Center for Meditation and Psychotherapy.

Jung, C.G. 'Quotable Quote.' Available at www.goodreads.com/quotes/485998, accessed on 18 November 2016.

Meditation 12: Life as a Painful Gift

Barks, C. and Moyne, J. (translators) (2004 [1273]) *The Essential Rumi – New Expanded Edition*. San Francisco, CA: HarperOne. [Rumi]

Bulley, C. (1994) *Glimpses of the Divine*. Eastbourne: The Alpha Press Ltd, an imprint of Sussex Academic Print. [Helen Keller]

Thich Nhat Hanh (2014) *No Mud, No Lotus*. Berkeley, CA: Parallax Press, p.13.

Meditation 14: Quaker Meeting for Worship

(2009) *Quaker Faith and Practice, Fourth Edition*. Chapter 27, Section 27.27. London: Quaker Peace & Service. [Isaac Penington]

Meditation 15: The Heart as a Lonely Hunter

Anonymous (2009) *The Chandogya Upanishad*. In S. Prabhavananda and F. Manchester (translators) *The Upanishads: Breath from the Eternal*. New York: Signet Classics.

Maharshi, R. (2009) 'Obsessive Burning Desires (Part 1) – Spoken by Mooji.' Available at www.youtube.com/watch?v=1qZ5elPuVEc&feature=youtube, accessed on 18 November 2016.

Dass, R. (ed.) (2005) *Paths to God: Living the Bhagavad Gita*. New York: Three Rivers Press/Crown Publishing Group. [Prophet Muhammed]

Meditation 16: What Desire Are You Using to Give Up Desire?

Mascaró, J. (2008) *Bhagavad Gita* (translated by L.L. Patton). London/ NewYork: Penguin. [St John of the Cross]

Soul Food (2010) 'Words of Wisdom.' Available at https:// dontmindnomind.wordpress.com/tag/ram-dass, accessed on 5 February 2017. [Ram Dass]

Lamott, A. (2005 [1994]) *Operating Instructions: A Journal of My Son's First Year*. London: Bloomsbury Publishing PLC/Anchor.

Vyasa, V. (2008) *The Bhagavad Gita* (translated by L.L. Patton). London/ New York: Penguin Group. [Krishna]

Meditation 17: The Light Dressed up as 'Self' and 'Other'

Anonymous (2009) *The Chandogya Upanishad*. In S. Prabhavananda and F. Manchester (translators) *The Upanishads: Breath from the Eternal*. New York: Signet Classics.

Watts, A. (2003 [1995]) *Become What You Are*. Boston, MA: Shambhala, p.44. [Arthur Eddington]

Watts, A. (1989 [1966]) *The Book: On the Taboo Against Knowing Who You Are*. New York: Vintage Books, p.15.

Meditation 18: The Mystery of Prayer

Pascal, B. 'Quotable Quote.' Available at www.goodreads.com/ quotes/559339-the-heart-has-its-reasons-which-reason-knows-nothing-of, accessed on 6 January 2016.

Tulsidas, G. (2016) *Tulsidas Ramayana*. Available at www.bhaktiware. com, accessed on 18 November 2016 [click on Who is?> Hanuman>Ramayana].

Meditation 19: 'Being' in Uncertainty

Solnit, R. (2006 [2005]) *A Field Guide to Getting Lost*. Edinburgh: Canongate, p.6.

Meditation 20: Waiting in the Light

Ambler, R.

Fox, G. (1653) 'Epistle 34.' In *The Works of George Fox* 7:42 [also in Ambler's anthology of George Fox, *Truth of the Heart*, Quaker Books, 2nd edition, 2007, 1:68].

Frankl, V.E. (2004 [1946]) *Man's Search for Meaning*. London: Rider.

Meditation 21: Whisper 'Yes'

Faulds, D. (2003) *One Soul: More Poems from the Heart of Yoga*. Greenville, VA: Peaceable Kingdom Books, 'White Dove'.

Meditation 22: The Play of Darkness and Light

Pagels, E. (1989 [1979]) *The Gnostic Gospels*. New York: Vintage Books, Gospel of Thomas, Verse 70, pp.xii–xxiii.

Zweig, C. and Abrams, J. (eds) (1991 [1990]) *Meeting the Shadow – The Hidden Power of the Dark Side of Human Nature*. New York: Tarcher/Penguin. [Carl Jung]

Vyasa, V. (2016) 'Digging up our divinity.' Available at www.ramdass.org/digging-up-our-divinity, accessed on 18 November 2016.

Meditation 23: Dancing with Fear

Rilke, R.M. (ed.) (2001) *Letters to a Young Poet* (translated by S. Mitchell). New York: Random House Inc.

Chödrön, P. (2005 [2003]) *When Things Fall Apart*. London: Element, p.5.

Meditation 24: Divine Play of Father and Son

Vyasa, V. (2008) *The Bhagavad Gita 2.12* (translated by L.L. Patton). London/New York: Penguin Group.

Baba, M. (1995) *Discourses*, 7th edition. Myrtle Beach, SC: Sheriar Foundation, pp.8–9.

Meditation 25: Going Underground

Medaglia, M. (2015) *One Year Wiser: 365 Illustrated Meditations*. London: SelfMadeHero. [Rainer Maria Rilke]

Meditation 26: Dropping Your Anchor

Star, J. (translator) (2003 [2001]) *Tao Te Ching – The New Translation from Tao Te Ching: The Definitive Edition*. New York: Penguin Group. [Lao Tzu]

Meditation 27: Laughter as a Doorway

Zocchi, M. (2011) *Zen Wisdom and Other Masters*. Melbourne: Brolga Publishing Pty Ltd. [Lao Tzu]

Blake, W. (2000 [1994]) *The Selected Poems of William Blake*. Ware: Wordsworth Editions Limited, 'Eternity'.

Chilton, A.M. (2016) 'Laughter: The closest thing to grace.' Available at https://billygraham.org/story/laughter-the-closest-thing-to-grace, accessed on 18 November 2016. [Karl Barth]

Meditation 28: Entrusting Yourself to the Waves

Stevens, J. (translator) (2006) *One Robe, One Bowl, The Zen Poetry of Ryokan.* Boulder, CO: Weatherhill Inc. [Ryokan]

Laird, M. (2011) *A Sunlit Absence: Silence, Awareness, and Contemplation.* New York: Oxford University Press. [Meister Eckhart]

Meditation 29: The Shadowlands

Starnes, T. (2014) *No One Knows When It's a Good Day.* Bloomington, IN: AuthorHouse. [Meister Eckhart]

Gasslein, B. (ed.) (2001 [1997, in French]) *How to Befriend Your Shadow.* Ottawa/London: Novalis/Darton, Longman & Todd Ltd. [Carl Jung, as quoted by J. Monbourquette]

Meditation 30: A Wounded Tree Still Blossoms

Rilke, R.M. (2010) *Duino Elegies: The Sonnets to Orpheus.* New York: Vintage Books.

Meditation 31: Eating Poppies with the Dead

Rilke, R.M. (1989 [1982]) *The Selected Poetry of Rainer Maria Rilke* (edited and translated by S. Mitchell). New York: Vintage International/Random House, 'The Turning Point'.

Réa, R. (2009) *Beyond Brokenness.* Bloomington, IN: Xlibris Corporation Publishers, 'The Unbroken'.

Meditation 32: The Ocean and the Waves

Harvey, A. (1995) *The Return of the Mother.* Berkeley, CA: North Atlantic Books. [Rumi]

Sri Nisargadatta (1992 [1973]) *I Am That: Talks with Sri Nisargadatta Maharaj.* Bombay: Chetana Press.

Mediation 33: The Mountain of Truth

Hanaford, P.A. (2005 [1883]) *Daughters of America or The Women of the Century.* New York: Cosimo Inc. [Lucretia Mott]

Shakespeare, W. (1990 [1982]) *The Complete Works of William Shakespeare: Romeo and Juliet, Act II, Scene II.* London: Hennewood Publications Ltd.

Galison, P.L., Holton, G. and Schweber, S.S. (eds) (2008) *Einstein for the 21st Century – His Legacy in Science, Art, and Modern Culture.* Princeton, NJ/Woodstock, Oxfordshire: Princeton University Press. [Albert Einstein]

Meditation 34: The Gift of Not Knowing

Johnson, T.H. (ed.) (1976) *The Complete Poems of Emily Dickinson*. New York: Amereon Limited (Faber Paperbacks). [Emily Dickinson]

Berry, W. (2011 [1983]) *Standing by Words: Essays*. Berkeley, CA: Counterpoint Press, 'The Real Work'.

Matthew 16.25. [Jesus]

Meditation 35: The Seeker

Lambdin, O. (translator) *Gospel of Thomas. 2*. Gnostic Society Library/ Nag Hammadi Library. Available at http://gnosis.org/naghamm/ gthlamb.html, accessed on 8 February 2017.

Lawrence, D.H. (2002 [1994]) *The Complete Poems of D.H. Lawrence*. Ware: Wordsworth Editions.

Meditation 36: The Sacred Heart of Jesus

Meyer, M. (ed.) (2009) *The Nag Hammadi Scriptures: The Revised and Updated Translation of Sacred Gnostic Texts*. San Francisco, CA: HarperOne. [Gospel of Thomas]

Galatians 2.19–20. [Saint Paul]

Meditation 37: The Infinite Sky Within

Das, K. (2010) *Chants of a Lifetime: Searching for a Heart of Gold*. London: Hay House UK Ltd. [Sri Ramakrishna]

Vyasa, V. (2013) *Bhagavad Gita, The Song of God, 6.30* (commentary by S. Mukundananda). Plano, TX: Jagadguru Kripaluji Yog.

Meditation 38: 'Being' En Route

Groth, M. (2016) *After Psycho Therapy*. Raleigh, NC: Lulu Press, Inc. [Meister Eckhart]

Meditation 39: Autism… It's Not What You Think

Damon, S.F. (1988) *A Blake Dictionary: The Ideas and Symbols of William Blake*. Hanover: Dartmouth College Press. [William Blake]

Dass, R. (2013) *Polishing the Mirror: How to Live from your Spiritual Heart*. Louisville, CO: Sounds True Inc. [Albert Einstein]

Chang, L. (ed.) (2006) *Wisdom for the Soul: Five Millennia of Prescriptions for Spiritual Healing*. Washington, DC: Gnosophia Publishers. [Oscar Wilde]

Meditation 40: Nothing Special

Lee Boyer, A. (2009) *Buddha on the Backstretch: The Spiritual Wisdom of Driving 200 mph*. Macon, GA: Mercer University Press, p.65. [Zen proverb]

Thich Nhat Hanh (2014) *No Mud, No Lotus*. Berkeley, CA: Parallax Press.

Meditation 41: There Is Nothing New

Ecclesiastes 1.9. (2015) *Holy Bible New Living Translation*. Illinois, IL: Tyndale House Publishers.

Davis, R.E. (2001 [1996]) *The Eternal Way: The Inner Meaning of the Bhagavad Gita 5.8*. Delhi: Motilal Banarsidass Publishers Private Limited. [V. Vyasa]

Meditation 42: ...and then, the Blackbird Sings

Franklin, R.W. (ed.) (1999) *Poems of Emily Dickinson*. Cambridge, MA: Harvard University Press. [Emily Dickinson]

Huxley, A. (2009 [1962]) *Island*. New York: Random House Inc.

Mascaró, J. (2008) *Bhagavad Gita* (translated by L.L. Patton). London/ NewYork: Penguin.

Meditation 43: Being an Elder

(2013) *Quaker Faith and Practice, Fifth Edition*. Chapter 10, Section 10.01. London: Quaker Books. [Isaac Penington, 1667]

Hoffman, J. (2008) 'Thoughts on eldering.' Available at www. inwardlight.org/2008/11, accessed on 18 November 2016. [Danelle LaFlower]

Meditation 44: Allowing Messiness

Parachin, V.M. (2013) *Sit a Bit: Five-Minute Meditations for Greater Health, Harmony and Happiness*. Huntsville, AZ: Ozark Mountain Publishing. [Lao Tzu]

Meditation 45: Healing the Wounds of Separation

Rumi, J. 'Quotable Quote.' Available at www.goodreads.com/ quotes/103315, accessed on 18 November 2016.

Winnicott, D.W. (1971) *Playing and Reality*. London: Tavistock Publications Ltd.

Meditation 46: A Doorway into Truth

Poonja, Sri H.W.L. (2000) *The Truth Is*. Boston, MA: Weiser Books. [Kabir]

Sadhu, M. (1974 [1957]) *In Days of Great Peace*. Hollywood, CA: Wiltshire Book Company. [Ramana Maharshi]

Meditation 47: Spiritual Bypassing

Caplan, M. (2011) *The Guru Question: The Perils and Rewards of Choosing a Spiritual Teacher.* Louisville, CO: Sounds True Inc. [Old Persian saying]

Dass, Ram, 'Phoney holy', in 'Living Spirit, Open Heart', Part 1 [talk], and 'You're in school', in 'Living Spirit, Open Heart', Part 2 [talk]. Available at www.dontmindnomind.wordpress.com/tag/ram-dass, accessed on 6 January 2017.

Meditation 48: Dancing with the Elephant in the Room

Moore, T. (1992) *Care of the Soul.* New York: HarperCollins.

Meditation 49: Autism as an Awakening

Kwok, M., Palmer, M. and Ramsay, J. (translators) (1994) *Tao Te Ching – The New Translation.* Dorset/Rockport, MA/Brisbane: Element Books Limited. [Lao Tzu]

Confucius. 'Quotable Quote.' Available at www.goodreads.com/quotes/106313, accessed on 18 November 2016.

Meditation 50: The Second Arrow

'The story of the second arrow.' Available at www.sharitaylor.com/blog/the-story-of-the-second-arrow, accessed on 18 November 2016. [Buddhist saying]

Meditation 51: Coming Home to 'Being'

Johnson, T.H. (ed.) (1976) *The Complete Poems of Emily Dickinson.* New York: Amereon Limited (Faber Paperbacks). [Emily Dickinson]

Meditation 52: Thought for the Day

The Brihadaranyaka Upanishad, IV.4.5. Inspirational Quotes. Available at www.inspirational-quotes.info/dest1.html, accessed on 26 November 2016.

Meditation 53: You Are the Music

Nietzsche, F. (loosely attributed to). Quote Investigator. Available at http://quoteinvestigator.com/2012/06/05/dance-insane, accessed on 6 February 2017.

Crombie, J. (ed.) (2016) *The Best Alan Watts Quotes.* Raleigh, NC: Lulu Press Inc. [Alan Watts]

Meditation 54: Sweet Etty Hillesum

Pomerans, A.J. (translator) (1996 [1981]) *Etty Hillesum, An Interrupted Life – The Diaries 1941–1943 and Letters from Westerbork*. New York: Owl Books, Henry Holt & Company.

Meditation 55: It's All Perfect

Pomerans, A.J. (translator) (1996 [1981]) *Etty Hillesum, An Interrupted Life: The Diaries 1941–1943 and Letters from Westerbork*. New York: Owl Books, Henry Holt & Company.

Aitken, R. (no date) 'Dubious quotes and stories attributed to Shunryu Suzuki.' Available at www.cuke.com/Cucumber%20Project/lectures/dubious.htm, accessed on 18 November 2016.

Meditation 57: It's All an Open Secret

Anonymous (2007) *The Upanishads* (translated by E. Easwaran). India: Nilgiri Press.

Kwok, M., Palmer, M. and Ramsay, J. (translators) (1994) *Tao Te Ching – The New Translation*. Dorset/Rockport, MA/Brisbane: Element Books Limited. [Lao Tzu]

Meditation 58: Eternally Grateful

Chesterton, G.K. (1986) *Collected Works: Volume 1*. San Francisco, CA: Ignatius Press.

Meditation 59: The Life that Never Ends

(2013) *Quaker Faith and Practice, Fifth Edition*. Chapter 22, Section 22.95. London: Quaker Books. [William Penn, 1693]

Hartel, D. and Sharma, A.K. (eds) (1991) Talks with Sri Ramana Maharshi, *The Maharshi*, May/June, 1, 2, Part 3, 'Death and dying.' New York: Ramana Maharshi Centre.

Meditation 60: The End of Words

March, S.J. (2015) *Fuel for Pilgrims, Volume 1*. Raleigh, NC: Lulu Press Inc., p.78. [St Thomas Aquinas]

Christopher Goodchild, the author of *A Painful Gift*, is a Quaker and spiritual teacher, with a deep interest in Eastern philosophy. He is an Ambassador for the National Autistic Society and lives in London. He loves walking aimlessly, birdwatching and being in bed each night by 9.10pm.

Julie Lonneman, a freelance illustrator, lives and works in Cincinnati, Ohio, where she maintains a studio. Her illustrations on themes of spirituality and social justice have appeared in magazines such as *America*, *Sojourners*, and *St Anthony Messenger*, and have graced the covers of numerous books and newsletters. An amazingly versatile artist, Julie works in many media and styles, but she is best known for her black and white scratchboard images and her coloured pencil illustrations.

.